HOW TO BE SELF-RELIANT IN...

THE MUSIC BUSINESS

WRITTEN BY

JULIA KUGEL & SCOTT MONTOYA

HAPPY SUNDAYS BOOKS
2026

We want to thank
Mick Boggis, David Dickenson, Andy Factor, JP Plunier,
Mom and Mom and Dad,
and all our friends and colleagues.

HOW TO BE SELF-RELIANT IN THE MUSIC BUSINESS

Like the music business, this book may not be suitable for children.
The concepts and ideas in this book are the opinions of the authors.
Do additional research before making any major life choices.
We aren't responsible for your decisions.
Good luck!

We didn't receive money for the endorsements in this book. In fact,
we give money to most of the companies we mention.
Think about *that*.

NO AI No AI was used in the creation of this book.

Thanks Masyafi Studio for letting us use their font *Morvanh.*

Illustrations by Scott Montoya.

First edition
ISBN - 979-8-9948987-0-3
Happy Sundays Books

Audiobook available

howtobeselfreliant.com

TABLE OF CONTENTS

No book can teach you everything you need to know, especially about being a musician, but the information in this book will save you time, money, stress and heartache.

Julia and I don't have degrees in music business. We started as untrained, unqualified amateurs with zero experience/previous resources/connections in the music industry and built our careers from the ground up. This book is about the knowledge and wisdom we've gained during our twenty-plus years in the biz.

BANDS

A band is a business that usually consists of people that have zero experience or knowledge of business, aka a ticking time bomb. Like any business, there's risk involved and the better equipped you are the less the chance of it all blowing up in your face. It's a lifestyle that requires a 24/7/365 commitment. You miss birthdays and weddings and family gatherings, basically anything important to anyone else. It takes at least one person a whole lot of time and energy with minimal returns for the first ten years. If you go all-in, you'll be broke, sleeping on floors, barely breaking even on tour and spending all your free time trying to grow your career with nothing to fall back on. It's a jungle out there. Learn the skills of survival or you'll be eaten alive.

Why it's important to have skills other than an instrument or voice:

Tasks that you outsource - whether it's booking shows, making merch, optimizing search engines, etc. - are things you can and should have a basic understanding of. This allows you to have more control, save tons of money, and spend less time waiting for someone to get back to you. Plus, there's less chance of getting screwed over. As an artist, certain things (like mastering your music and proofreading contracts) are best handled by professionals, but the rest can be achieved by those willing to learn.

WHAT THIS BOOK ISN'T

This isn't a comprehensive guide to music theory. This isn't a step-by-step guide to success. This book is not going to tell you how to "get" an agent, a manager, signed by a record label, more subscribers or followers, likes or views, your music on playlists, beat the algorithm, make your mixes pop, or make people like you. I can't tell you how to get the cheese, but I can tell you what the traps look like.

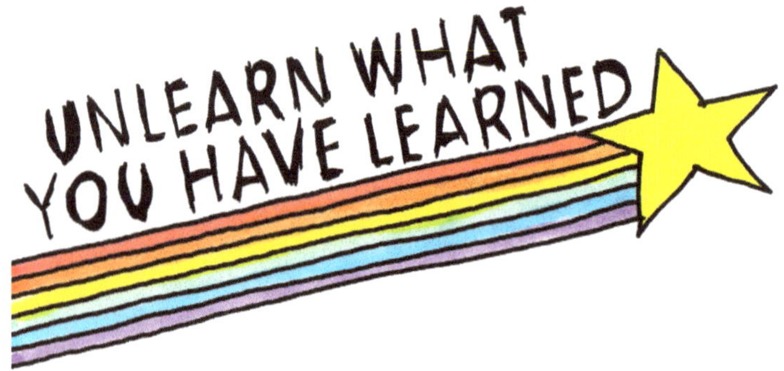

The world is full of misconceptions, and the general view of the life of a musician is no exception. We all glamourize the life of a musician thanks to the stories that we see in movies and TV, it's what attracts so many people to the lifestyle. A common misunderstanding about music life is that popularity equals wealth. That may be the case with giant artists, but those are the rare exceptions. Another misunderstanding is that bands are always happy and confident and nothing is ever wrong because they are successful. People smile in photos, but there's more to a general state of mind than a fraction of a second. Photographs don't show the whole picture. Music has way more to it than being in a nice studio and on a giant stage. The music life is all encompassing, generally unstable, inconsistent and insecure. There's no road map to success and no guarantee that anything you do will work out.

Some people have millions of dollars in the bank, mansions and boats and still aren't happy. The music life can make you money, sure, but so can working a 9-5 in a cubicle. What this lifestyle really offers are the experiences you'll have, the people you'll meet, the countries you'll visit and the things you'll learn. If you're lucky, work hard, don't sign away your rights and register your tracks correctly, you might get some royalty checks too. Figure out what your definition of success is and be ok with whatever happens.

WHAT IS AN ARTIST?

The band or artist is the *talent*, the centerpiece of a production. The main ingredient, the reason everything else around it exists. Often, artists are paid the least and don't have control over their own lives. Harsh criticism, scrutiny, and judgement are part of the job description. If you make it to a certain level, even your safety can be at risk. Some artists end up getting treated as products rather than humans.

A green musician is like a child, innocent, naive, willing to believe anything, driven by the need to create. The reality is that the music business is cutthroat and ruthless. Be aware of the dark side so you can protect yourself. Expand your definition of *artist* to include the left-brain aspects of the business. Familiarizing yourself with these concepts will decrease your chances of becoming another casualty. The most successful artists have learned to diversify their skillsets to create their own value.

THERE'S NO SUCH THING AS INSTANT SUCCESS

You have to pay your dues, no way around that. It's going to take ten years of hard work, releasing music and touring before you notice any significant return on your investment.

THERE ARE THREE BYPRODUCTS OF A HUMAN LIFE: ART, CHILDREN AND TRASH.

If you can talk, you can play music. The movements of the lungs, diaphragm, tongue and lips make the respiratory system a very intricate instrument used to communicate ideas. So for anyone that says they can't play music, just the fact that they said that negates their claim. Not only can they play, but they're masters of their instrument.

Art is a curation of ingredients that come together to communicate something. Music is curated sounds, painting is curated paint, dancing is curated movements. How do we reach the end result? A series of decisions! How do we make those decisions? By using our *artistic intuition*. Try to develop this intuition. Look around and assess how the things you see resonate with your subconscious. Spend some time looking at mugshots and see how you feel. Smear some paint on a piece of paper and see if that shape makes you feel happy or sad or calm or confused. Move objects around on a table until the *composition* makes sense to you. Typefaces (fonts) are some of my favorite things in the whole world. They have a very subtle way of communicating.

Which of these fonts communicate this message the best?

My name is Scott and I like to drink blood.

MY NAME IS SCOTT AND I LIKE TO DRINK BLOOD.

My name is Scott and I like to drink blood.

The answer is: all of them. Fonts are as effective for communicating as the words themselves. The first one is kinda off-putting and uncomfortable; your brain can't really place it. The middle one is kinda on the nose and the third one looks like some sort of ad for a medical device that takes your blood named Scott for some reason. Fonts are great, spend more time with them. Julia says there's no difference between Helvetica and Arial but she's wrong…

DEAD WRONG.

EXPAND YOUR INFLUENCES

Humans involuntarily copy the things they experience. Your art is an amalgamation of everything that inspires you. Having a vast collection of influences to draw on will make your art more interesting. That includes architecture, science, literature, ancient mosaics, etc. Interesting art is made by interesting people.

FTW

One of my favorite stories of art is when Michelangelo was painting *The Last Judgement* in the Sistine Chapel. The original painting had majority of the figures depicted as nudes which really upset a cardinal named Biagio da Cesena, who complained about the nudity to the Pope. Offended by the attempt at censorship, Michelangelo painted the cardinal as a character from Greek mythology who judged dead people in the underworld, complete with donkey ears and some nice snake underwear. When the cardinal complained once again, the Pope said that Hell was out of his jurisdiction so there was nothing he could do. The cardinal is memorialized as the biggest jackass in hell but at least he's not naked. A lot of meaning can be extracted from this exchange, but the main point is that censorship sucks and so do critics. Don't be afraid to express yourself, that's the whole point of art. PS, Michelangelo's self-portrait in that painting is epic.

WABI SABI

Wabi Sabi is a Japanese philosophy about aesthetic. Everything is in a constant state of growth or decay, and the perfection is in the imperfections. This translates to music because no performance or recording is going to be perfect to everyone. Character is what makes art human. It's the flaws in the diamond that make it sparkle.

BIG DECISIONS

The thing I like most about Bob Ross is when he makes *big decisions*. He will spend 20 minutes painting a beautiful mountain and a stream and some happy little trees and then take a big brush with black paint and make a huge slash down the middle of it, paint some branches on that slash and *bam* it's a tree in the foreground.

HAPPY ACCIDENTS

These are the best. Distortion or a glitch or a spill or something breaks and sends the whole project in a new direction or adds the finishing touch you were looking for. Keep an open mind, accidents can be gifts. Let the art become a collaborator in its own creation.

CULTURE = PEOPLE COPYING PEOPLE

Musicians generally want their music to become popular, but popularity is a strange concept because it has nothing to do with quality. It's counterproductive to base your own opinion of your music on its perceived popularity. Some bands get huge right away; some take a little longer if they ever do. It's all about how you feel about what you're doing. If only a few people come to your show, don't mistake that for a lack of talent. Understanding trends is a good way to understand how the general public operates and will give you another perspective on what's actually happening.

Culture and trends are the same thing. To understand them, let's start with the basics. People see another person behaving a certain way, subconsciously agree or disagree, and take on a form of that behavior in a constant state of attraction and repulsion. These behaviors add up to a trend, a fad, a movement or just "the way it is". When people see something they don't like, they act inversely and when they see something they like, they copy it. Food trends, workout trends, clothing trends, trends of ideas, speech patterns, ways of living; these are all mimicked behaviors. I grew up in southern California, so the way I talk is different than if I grew up in Scotland. Same language (kinda), but my speech pattern had different influences.

DON'T BLAME THE BEE GEES

Trends that go mainstream tend to get caricatured and misunderstood, often to the detriment of the original idea. In the 1970's, an underground African American/Latino/gay dance club movement called disco was growing in popularity. The film *Saturday Night Fever* propelled disco into the mainstream where it was misconstrued and over-commercialized. The movement promoting freedom, liberation and great music soon turned into a kitschy costume party with a sub-par soundtrack. Oversaturation fueled resentment which resulted in a pile of records getting blown up in front of 50,000 people at a major league baseball game in Chicago. RIP disco.

The big question of a trend is do people actually like it, or do they like it because other people like it? Did they stop liking it because other people stopped liking it? Are things good because they're popular? Are they popular because they're good? Are people that follow trends just… posers? Swing pops up as a trend now and then, is swing something that was missing from people's lives and then they discover it and start dressing and talking all swing, or are they just following the trend? Did people in Rococo-era France put on tights and a wig and big poofy sleevey thing because that was an expression of their individuality and their belief in personal freedom?

Society has many forces of influence, some are blatant and some are unnoticeable, but never fall into the trap of thinking of anything as "normal". It's a dangerous word. "Common" is a more fitting description of contemporary long-term trends. It's common for people to own a smart phone. Saying it's *normal* to own a smart phone comes off pretty stuck-up. People can do/say/be anything they want to be, common or uncommon. Normal has nothing to do with it.

It's common for a musician to want to gain a following and turn their talent into a career, but is it common for a musician to want to go mainstream? Is it possible to go mainstream without watering down your style? Is going mainstream *selling out*? Is this something you want for yourself?

Here's a few types of trends I've noticed:

IN SIGHT IN MIND

People eat what they're fed, and companies pay a lot of money for space in that bucket. Most things you hear and see aren't there by accident, they're strategically placed for the general public to gorge themselves on. Since humans are easy to manipulate and imitate everything they see, what they're consuming gets incorporated into their personality, fashion, beliefs and general outlook on life. For instance, when a dog is featured in a movie, that dog breed sees a surge in demand. *Beverly Hills Chihuahua* came out in 2008, and Chihuahua sales boomed for a while.

THE PENDULUM

This theory has two roads leading to the same place. First is the ebb and flow of nature. Tides rise and fall, day becomes night becomes day, winter turns into summer. Next time you're lying down, notice how long it takes you to adjust positions. After a while of having straight legs, they start to kinda hurt so you bend them, and the cycle continues. When you're hot, cold feels good. When you're cold, hot feels good. After a while, everything starts to cramp up and needs to change. Society flows like this too. The exclusivity of hair metal getting replaced by the accessibility of grunge was a great example of that.

Newton's Third Law of Motion states that "every action has an equal and opposite reaction," and I've noticed that Social Physics operates in the same way. Every action will have its opposite reaction (though not always equal). Elvis Presley's manager, capitalizing on The King's surge in popularity, made a killing selling buttons that say, "I HATE ELVIS".

Trends are on a pendulum that is constantly swinging. If you can get ahead of this pattern you can set yourself up for success, most likely by selling "I HATE (insert subject here)" merch. People are so predictable it's boring. Just remember, the antithesis of a thing is still that thing, so if that thing is (or isn't) your thing, you're still connected with that thing. Try operating outside the realm of whatever mass hysteria is taking hold at that moment. It's a much more subtle pendulum to ride and you won't get as much attention but at least you'll be thinking for yourself.

15 MINUTES

Short-term novelties that disappear as quickly as they appear, sometimes earning a nickname and a manager. Social media *challenges* fall into this category, often challenging (peer pressuring) people to do stupid shit that might be harmful to themselves or others. Gender reveal parties are another trend that isn't quite alive but isn't quite dead either, but I'd still classify as short-term. Food and diet trends are another silly way to conform, things like doing the water/maple syrup/cayenne pepper fasting thing and eating Tide Pods.

GRADUAL INTEGRATION

Selfies are a perfect example of a trend that has started and integrated itself in my lifetime. At one point, taking a selfie was generally seen as pretty embarrassing. Then people saw other people taking selfies, tiptoed into it, now it's just something people do. Social media has the world starting to merge into one big cultural blob. Halloween has creeped into the global routine too, creating tons of unnecessary single use plastic trash each year.

MARKETING TRENDS

Corporations closely monitor trends to incorporate into their marketing campaigns, and being on trend is a great way to relate to the masses. "We're one of you! Ask your doctor about…" There are trends in marketing styles that drive me up the f-in wall, things like "Very. Big. Deal." and "Yea, we did that". Commercials that feature home movies of touching moments shot on phones set to sentimental music are another disgusting way of manipulating people to buy a product.

Even if they aren't aware of it, most people are following trends. It's important to question all your behavior and assess whether you're being true to yourself, an unquestioning slave to society afraid to step outside the box for fear of rejection, or just a trendy poser. Understanding trends can make you care less about what people think because lots of people don't even know what they think or why they think it.

Playing an instrument, whether it's your voice or something outside yourself, is an incredible expression of your own human experience. There are methods, scales, classes, and philosophies for every instrument, but the best thing to do is simply to start! "I can't" should be flushed from your vocabulary. The *10,000-hour rule* is the theory that it takes 10,000 hours of playing to become an expert. The sooner you start racking those hours up the better! Playing new instruments helps expand your creative process. Say you typically write songs on guitar, try banging around on a piano or drums. You may write songs from a whole new perspective when you change the scene. New vocal patterns or melodies may emerge when you get out of your habitual playing patterns. No matter what instrument you play, practice to a metronome!

WEAR EARPLUGS!

Especially during practice and soundcheck! Feedback from monitors and amps can cause major damage to your ears. This is called *tinnitus* and it's super annoying. You are going to need your hearing!! I learned this lesson too late after damaging my right ear. Also move off the stage or away from monitors when sound engineers say they are going to *ring out* the monitors. Feedback can temporarily or permanently damage your hearing. It's smart to get a headphone mixer for practice too. This allows everyone to hear themselves and you don't have to blast your instruments to be louder than the drums.

VOCALS

If you plan on singing for a career, get in the habit of warming up before performances. A simple warm up can save you from losing your tone and range. Consult a vocal coach at least once for warmup techniques and best practices. You can also find some ideas online. Serious damage can occur on vocal cords if they are improperly treated. Simple exercises such as lip trills loosen the tension in your mouth and help prevent strain. Alcohol is bad for your vocal cords; room temperature water is best. If you do consume alcohol before you play, pair it with plenty of water and vocal warmups. Talking before and after shows in noisy environments may be the worst thing you can do if you are a vocalist. People usually want to chat after a show and that extra push can really strain the throat. After a performance, it is best to do vocal cool downs, drink water and let your voice rest. Trust me - when your voice is young and resilient it may not seem like this is important but fifteen years down the line you may regret not getting into better habits early on. Do yourself a favor and take care of your instrument before damage is done.

GUITAR

Try different guitars and different pick thicknesses. Explore! Try out different gear and see what clicks. Short scale guitars are awesome if you are of a smaller stature or like the ease of having frets closer together. Your playing style is the number one way of differentiating you from everyone else. Listen to your intuition while developing your sound. The way I picked my amp - when I was finally able to upgrade - was by bringing my own guitar to the music store, plugging into every amp one at a time, and standing back to see if the sound moved me. Pedals are cool and everything, but they break, and you should be able to play your set no matter what. They should elevate your existing sound rather than *being* your sound. Nothing shows mastery more than someone who plays well through a simple set up. Let the extra stuff just be extra.

DRUMMING

Drumming is a unity of mind and body. You gotta be able to count, stay on beat, anticipate anything fancy you're gonna do and not drop a stick while doing it. It's challenging! Pick up a book of rudiments, a physical book not something on a phone. *Stick Control for The Modern Snare Drummer* by George Lawrence Stone is a good one, but there's plenty more out there. Download a metronome app and start at 40bpm, focusing on your technique and grip. Slowly go through the motions on each pattern until your muscles memorize those movements. Drumming is all about muscle memory which means you have to practice a LOT. Always count out loud when practicing and don't get tempted to speed up past the metronome. Sounds easier than it is. Any combo of rudiments can be put on any of your limbs and ghost notes and accents can be put on any of those hits. Fills are death traps for beats unless you're super confident. If you want to start playing fills, try cutting notes instead of adding. Instead of eighth notes, try half notes. Being consistent and stylish is way better than some fast and sloppy fill. You can ease into those when you're ready.

Drums need to be tuned too! Like every other instrument, they're more fun to play and sound better when they're in tune.

To get more dexterity in your non-dominant hand, go switch in daily life. Instead of eating and drinking with your right hand, use your left. Write, use chopsticks and open doors with your less-used hand. Get your other hand up to speed!

BASS

If you use your fingers to play, try using baby powder on both hands. On bass, there's no such thing as too smooth.

KEYBOARD

There are so many ways to manipulate sound with a keyboard it can be exciting and overwhelming. All the settings and routing options, pre-sets and pedals, samples and amps. Do you but please chill!

PERCUSSION

Percussion adds that extra texture that can change your performance from ordinary to classic. Many artists have elevated their songs with a tambourine, a cowbell, or claves. Percussion can add dimension to an average song. So grab a shaker and get shakin'!

BACKUP VOCALS

Harmonies can turn a good song into a great song.

MISC INSTRUMENTS

Don't be afraid to introduce a lap steel or a cello to your sound. From hardcore to indie to hip hop, utilizing interesting instrumentation is the key to individuality. Oftentimes the unexpected will garner greater attention and acclamation than doing the same thing everyone else does. Bang on stuff! Get weird! To a metronome!

NOT EVERY SONG NEEDS A BRIDGE

Unless you plan on being a career cover band, you will be writing your own songs. You may be inspired by other bands or artists but best to tell your own unique story. Write from your own experience - your own truth. Some folks start with lyrics, while others with melody.

Think of songs as totally independent beings that need their own nurturing and attention. Each is special and different and an opportunity to explore one of your emotions. The simplest way to start writing a song is just by playing one string, one note, or one beat and just tuning into your consciousness and your heart. Say whatever comes to mind. It's called stream of consciousness and it's how many poets and writers begin their work. In my experience songs come from the ether - you should catch them when inspiration strikes. That's why I always record the initial ideas or jams. The memo app on my phone has 1500 recordings - many of which have been turned into songs. If I have writers block, I randomly select one from these memos and work on that one. It's a great way to catalog and time stamp your songs and ideas. Saving ideas in an accessible place is crucial so you can go back in three years and realize that a discarded idea wasn't bad, your perspective on it just had to shift.

Don't limit your creativity. Don't hold back on songwriting or production because you don't think you'll be able to replicate it on stage. Albums will outlive us all and "I can't do this live so I'm not gonna put it on the record" isn't a very good argument. Recording and live performance are two different artforms, it's ok to treat them as such. Genres are dumb - it's counterproductive to box yourself in creatively.

SONG SPLITS

If you have a writing partner(s), make sure you address song credits. People can make a lot of assumptions about who wrote what and who deserves credit. Even a tambourine player could argue they wrote part of the song. This can lead to all kinds of problems so have this discussion before, during or directly after to avoid an uncomfortable situation. The best way is to put the agreed-to song splits in writing with a date. Email works great. A piece of paper with song name, date, writer's names & percentage of ownership, and signatures is ideal. Scan it in and email it to yourself and everyone involved. That way if the paper goes missing you still have it to reference. You will need the song split percentages when you register the song with your PRO (ASCAP, BMI, SESAC ETC). If the songwriters already belong to a PRO it would be great to include their IPIs on the sheet as well so that the correct people get the credit. More on registering your songs in the ROYALTIES chapter.

COPYRIGHT YOUR MUSIC AND BAND NAME

Make sure you protect yourself and copyright your music and band name. If it's not copyrighted it's up for grabs and if someone or something steals it, it can be a very expensive fight. Securing a copyright for your songs is especially important now with the blurred lines of what is AI digestible. Lawyers are expensive and litigation lawyers are VERY expensive. Lawsuits totally suck and can last for years so spend the $85 to copyright your music and band name.

COLLABORATION APPS

Collaboration apps are central databases for a project. They keep the song info, metadata, splits and listenable tracks in one place that everyone in the project has access to. They can export .rin files after a project too, more on that in the Metadata chapter.

Two of them that I like are:

Veva Collect
www.vevacollect.com

Session Studio
www.sessionstudio.com

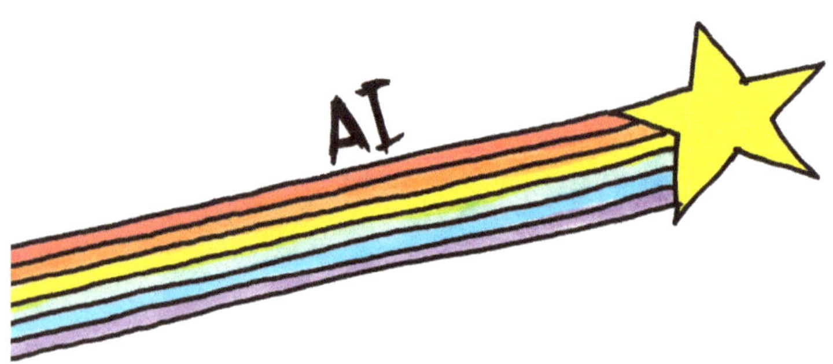

DON'T CHEAT YOURSELF

Humanity is on an endless quest for convenience. Like the airplane, email and GLP-1 receptor antagonists, AI is allowing people to conveniently use technology they don't understand to do things they would otherwise have a harder time doing. If your job is to constantly churn out content for the marketing department of a corporation then AI can be your best friend. If your goal is to survive on your art, it won't benefit you to cut corners. You should be constantly striving to be better, and the use of AI won't help you achieve that. Every step of the creative process has something to teach you. Every decision and mistake can change the end result drastically. Every project is practice for the next project.

Don't become reliant on a brain that isn't your own. Don't use AI to make songs, flyers, band logo, or anything your creativity would otherwise provide you with.

AI is a plagiarism machine. Make sure you protect your creations by copyrighting your music with the USPTO. There's a fee but it's better than getting ripped off. SACEM has a timestamp service called Musicstart (www.musicstart.com)

that will timestamp your tracks just in case you need to verify their creation date.

PEOPLE HAVE THE RIGHT TO KNOW WHAT THEY'RE PUTTING IN THEIR MINDS AS WELL AS THEIR BODIES.

We both strongly believe that if AI is used to create art, the consumers should be notified. Conversely if you don't use AI then you should label that as well. Think of it like a *vegan* or *gluten-free* mark. As of 2/7/2026, there's no standard mark for labelling art or music as AI-free. Here are two marks we've put on the last two records we've released, Julia Julia *Sugaring A Strawberry* and Soft Palms *In Echo*.

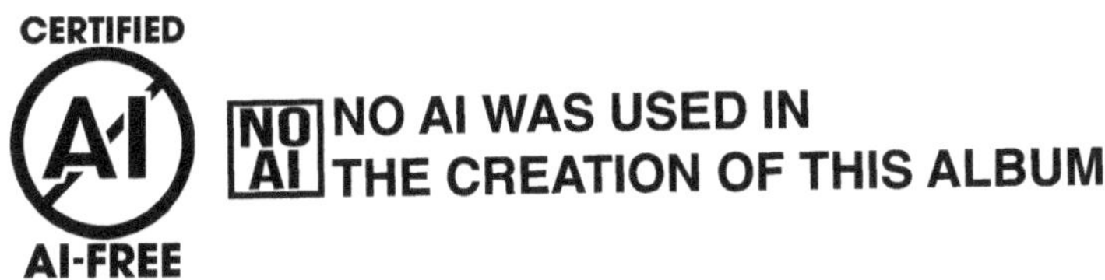

As AI becomes more ubiquitous it will be harder to differentiate human creativity from robot plagiarism. The use of AI to write music and lyrics is inevitable as generations are born into the common practice but just because everyone is doing it doesn't make it the right thing to do. My point is if you use ChatGPT or OpenAI to write lyrics or compose music you should let people know.

There's nothing DIY about using AI to make art or music. Besides, what happens when AI wants its writing royalties?

Recording can be one of the more stressful parts of music life. It's easy to get weighed down by the foreverness of it all. There are some simple things you can do to get ready for the studio. First, show up on time. Showing up on time is a show of respect for yourself and others. There is so much more involved in recording than just playing. The set-take part of recording can take a while, especially if you are using your own gear. Loading in, tuning, setting up mics and getting the sound right requires hours, maybe days of work. This can be cut down by using studio gear, which is usually tuned to the room and may even be already mic'd up. You might want to explore gear, instrument and mike options which equals time spent experimenting with sound before laying down tracks. Be patient and try to enjoy this portion of the process.

It really helps the situation if you don't show up drunk or hung over. Nothing worse than being confined in a small space with a belligerent fool. That kind of rockstar behavior is counterproductive and negatively affects the morale of the group. Those new to the business often think that being in the studio is an excuse to rage, but for the people working in the studio it is work. Have respect for those working to make your dreams come true. It's more fun if you are well rehearsed and can knock every song out first try. Engineers will love you and it will be overall a great experience. If you can't nail it by take three, you'll get all in your head and start getting frustrated and the takes probably won't get much better. Comping tracks (piecing together parts of different takes) is convenient and has been around since the beginning but dude, just nail it.

VOCAL RECORDING

Vocal recording tends to be the more high-stress part of the process. Typically, the band records the track first then vocals are tracked separately (unless the setup allows for a full live recording). This is done to minimize bleed on the vocal track. Record a scratch vocal or a vocal take early in the process to reference for arrangement and any additional instrumentation. The vocals often ground the song, so warm up, drink some room temp water or licorice tea and go in there and nail the vocals. Getting it off your plate early will help relieve the pressure and move the process along.

PRODUCERS

At some point you might want to work with a producer, which can have a few roles in creating a record. A producer can be a recording engineer, but not all recording engineers are producers. A producer is there to see the bigger picture, offer ideas for arrangement or orchestration and inspire an artist to give a great performance. They are the ones basically driving the bus so everyone else can relax and perform well. Some producers work with bands on the songwriting - a process called pre-production. This allows for everyone to be on the same page and create a more cohesive record. It's important to have meetings and discussions with your producer about the direction you want your music to take. To find a producer or engineer or studio, have a look at the credits of a song or album you like and reach out to whoever produced or recorded it. Discuss the role you want the producer to play, how involved you would like them to be and what you are trying to achieve. Be prepared to pay a fee and *points* on the record, which means giving up a portion of your royalties. That percentage could be 3-20% depending on the type of deal you agree to.

During the mixing process, each person will typically only listen to their own instrument. Bass players will only comment on the bass sound, tone, performance, etc. Same with drummers, guitarist, vocalist, keyboardist… you get the picture. Having another person in the room that is paying attention to the overall performance is super important. That person can be the engineer or a producer.

If you are self-producing, try to see the bigger picture and not just your part. If you're having the track mixed via the internet, put one person in charge of communicating with the mixing engineer. Have the whole band agree on the notes before sending them.

Everybody gets nervous about recording, even the most amazing players. Warm up and...

STUDIO ETIQUETTE

• DON'T WASTE STUDIO TIME. Don't ask the engineer any questions about how equipment works. If music is playing, someone is most likely listening to it. If you need to talk, leave the room and SHUT THE DOOR.

• Recording equipment is expensive and the settings are carefully dialed in. Don't touch anything.

• Don't blow into the microphone! That will break it.

• Change and tune your strings and drum heads before you go into the studio.

• It's a recording studio, not a rehearsal studio. You're there to take a sonic photograph, not to work out the songs. That should be worked out in pre-production. Know the BPM, key and key changes of each song.

• After the last hit on a take, don't talk or make noise for five seconds. Give the song a chance to end in silence.

• Don't eat or drink in the studio or control room.

• Have a pre-production meeting with the engineer beforehand to discuss what you'd like to accomplish and in what time frame. It will help make better use of the time in the studio when the clock is ticking.

Merch is a primary way to make money in music. A band logo is a form of branding. It's good marketing and can be the centerpiece of your merch universe. The trickiest part is formatting so learn to use a scanner and photo editing software like Photoshop and Illustrator. There is a free version called Canva that works too. Exposure to art helps you design more unique and interesting merch. There really are no rules, even a stupid doodle can make a good shirt.

SCREEN PRINTING

It took me way too long to start screen printing. It's easy and fun and saves lots of money. You can screen shirts, posters, patches, stickers, cd sleeves, record jackets, anything. You can try burning your own screens, but there's a learning curve. To get up and running, you're better off contacting a screen printing company and see if they will burn one for you. All they need is a black and white image. Start with a one-color design. Use acrylic ink and make sure to cure the ink in the dryer after it's dry to the touch. Search for bulk shirt websites and you can get shirts for $3-5. If you live near a fabric store, buy some fabric and screen some patches. You can screen your own patches and stickers with the same screen; just make sure you get the right ink for stickers.

HOW SCREEN PRINTING WORKS

Think of a screen as a stencil. A mesh screen is covered in a think paint-like substance called photo emulsion and left to dry. When exposed to UV light, the dry photo emulsion hardens (cures). Any area not exposed UV light won't cure, therefore can be removed (sprayed out with water), thus exposing bare areas of the screen that ink can pass through. Each screen is used to apply one color in a design. Designs with more than one color require multiple screens.

Screens come in different mesh counts. Ask a professional print shop what mesh count your project may require.

IMPORTANT: Screen print ink must be cured! Most inks need to be heated to a certain temperature for a specific amount of time. Just because the ink is dry to the touch doesn't mean it's cured! Uncured ink will turn back into liquid ink when washed and ruin all the other clothes in the washing machine. A regular clothes dryer on high heat can sometimes be used to cure water-based ink but READ THE INSTRUCTIONS on the container to make sure.

TYPES OF INK:
ACRYLIC (Water based)
PROS: Easy to clean up, just rinse out with water. Shirts can cure in the dryer. Laundromat dryers work great for curing ink, they get HOT
CONS: Dries fast on the screen, gotta keep production moving or else your design will get clogged by dry ink

PLASTISOL (PVC resin and plastic)
PROS: Doesn't dry until cured.
CONS: It's difficult to clean because it's not water-soluble.

Requires a special cleaning solution to remove from screen and equipment. CANNOT CURE IN DRYER. Requires a higher curing temperature.

ILLUSTRATIONS ON NEXT PAGE:

1. Photo emulsion applied to screen; transparency of design printed with center markers.

2. UV light "burns" the screen, all exposed photo emulsion hardens, the uncured stuff in the shade is sprayed out. Your design is now on the screen!

3. Mark a center line on your platen (flat surface that holds shirt/poster/thing you're printing on)

4. Align center marks on screen to center line on platen.

5. Screen it! Look up screen printing techniques and remember to flood the screen between pulls.

6. You have a shirt! Make sure you cure the ink.

7. You can screen patches and stickers too.

Steps 1 & 2 have a big learning curve, need lots of equipment and are best left to a professional when first starting out. Your time is better spent screening. Call a screen printing house or screen printing supply store and see if they will burn one for you. If you live in the Los Angeles / Orange County area, McLogan Supply is great.

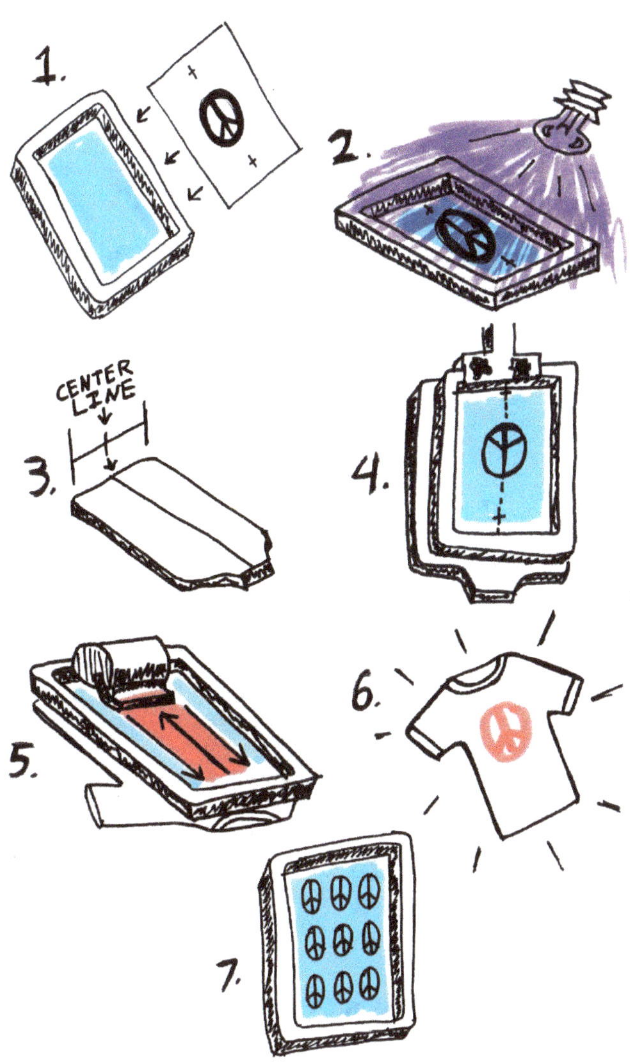
1.
2.
CENTER
LINE
3.
4.
5.
6.
7.

POS - POINT OF SALE (WHERE TO SELL MERCH)

IN PERSON

- Cash - Have small bills on hand for change.
- Square - Free to setup, charges a fee for each sale. www.squareup.com
- Venmo - Free cash app - www.venmo.com
- PayPal - We all know what PayPal is - www.paypal.com

ONLINE

- Bandcamp - www.bandcamp.com

You can sell music downloads and merch on Bandcamp, which also has show dates on your page. Takes a cut of each sale.

- Shopify - www.shopify.com

Has a $5/month plan and integration to YouTube, TikTok, Instagram and Facebook. Takes a cut of each sale. The customer service could be better.

MERCH ETIQUETTE

The merch area is usually limited, so don't hog the table. Always wait for the headliner to set up their merch even if you get there first.

Be creative in displaying your merch! Lights and quirky displays get more attention. Remember to bring basics like hangers, tape, marker and price list with QR code for easier selling.

Playing live is how a band finds its sound and builds a following. When you first start out, you'll have to book your own shows. You'll have better luck reaching out to an independent venue, meaning a venue not owned by a major promotion company like Live Nation, Goldenvoice and AEG Live. Independent venues are very important. 2020 came around and during that whole shutdown thing the big promotion companies bought up a bunch of independent venues. Corporate venues don't take chances on smaller bands the way independent venues do. House shows are on the rise too. Websites like freakscene.us are doing a great job at promoting DIY shows.

There are also independent promoters. Look at the top of a show flyer and it should say something like "PARADE OF FLESH PRESENTS". Find them on social media and reach out! I'm sure they would love to hear from you. Go to the shows they book and try to meet them! Check out the vibe! At least then you'll be supporting them and it's a much better look than sending an...

EPK (ELECTRONIC PRESS KIT)

We've never opened an EPK. Not once. People aren't likely

to open any random emails with attachments, especially if the emails are more than two sentences and besides, any email with an attachment is most likely going to spam. If you're emailing a promoter, keep it short! **Send a link to a video of a live show**. Not a music video, not a Spotify link, not an EPK, a live performance. Still, the best thing to do is to go to shows and…

MAKE FRIENDS

Music is a community and you want to know people in your local scene. **GO TO SHOWS. MEET PEOPLE. TALK TO EACH OTHER. SUPPORT EACH OTHER. COLLABORATE AND LEARN FROM EACH OTHER.** That's how great scenes are created, and great bands come out of great scenes.

Once you play some local shows the next step is to go on tour. Bring lots of socks and **GET A DOLLY**. It's smart to bring your own vocal mic because venue mics are disgusting. You're basically sharing a toothbrush with everyone that's ever played there.

A tree in a pot can only grow so big. If you're serious about music, you have to tour. Bands that are starting out should be ok with playing to one or two or no people, even if you have a big draw when you play in your hometown. You might think the first tour is going to be the stadium tour with screaming fans but that's most likely not the case.

When you're starting out, play as many shows as you can. There's more to playing music than just playing music. Think of performing as a form of practice. One hour of performing is the equivalent of 10 hours practicing alone. Be comfortable playing to just the sound guy. Get used to being on stage. Take all opportunities that present themselves to learn how shows usually flow and operate. Get good at line checks and playing under different conditions. A practical strategy is to go on tour and open for a bigger band (duh), then go back and play the same cities on your own a few months later while you're still fresh in people's brains.

OVERHEAD

Touring has a massive overhead. *Gross* profit is the big number, the one that looks great on paper until you see the cost for: bus or van rental, hotels, gas, flights, food, manager's commission, agent's commission, business manager's commission, tour manager fee, crew fee, merch cut from the venue, taxes. The money the artist gets, the leftover crumbs, that called *net,* but it's usually pretty gross.

KEEP TRACK OF YOUR MONEY!

At least one person should oversee counting all the money that goes in, all the money that goes out, and all the receipts. If you are that person, protect yourself from being accused of mismanaging money by copying as many band members on every email with the business manager as possible. If band members see lots of money coming in from tour and don't understand how much touring *actually* costs, there can be confusion on where that money went. Ignorance breeds anger and resentment. Keep your spreadsheets on a cloud server like Dropbox or Google Sheets so if your laptop and receipt scanner get stolen out of the bus in Nashville mid-tour, you'll have a backup of your work. If you have a company credit card, you can put a limit on how much each card carrier can spend. Be prepared to fill out a W-9 form or have one filled out in an online tour folder you can share with the promoter.

PROMOTERS

The promoter is the person who puts on the show and is responsible for paying you afterwards. Advancing the show means getting in touch with the promoter, and getting the times for load in, sound check, doors, set times, where to park, etc. This is also who you send a stage plot/input list, rider and press kit to, meaning a band pic and a show flyer that they should post at the venue or on the venue website. I don't recommend letting promoters handle the show flyer design. Make your own, just don't use AI to do it. Some venues have banned AI-generated show flyers, which I think is awesome. AI art sucks.

DOOR DEALS VS. GUARANTEES

Door deals are when a venue pays you for the amount of people who paid to get in. A guarantee is a flat fee for the band to play. These are all details that get hammered out with the promoter or the talent buyer at a venue. This can include a percentage of the bar and a bonus if it sells out. Sometimes they make you rent the room and add a room fee.

BACKLINE

Backline refers to a drum set and bass amp and maybe guitar amp that gets shared for the whole show, making changeovers between bands quicker and easier. Usually, the venue or festival will tell you to bring *breakables* (Kick pedal, cymbals, snare). If you're sharing backline and need to adjust the settings, take a picture of the settings and try to put them back to where they were. If the headliner is nice enough to let you use their gear, don't change anything. Deal with how it is. The bass tone is fine, and if the drummer is left-handed then guess what, so are you. Bringing your own cymbal stands, snare stand, hi-hat stand and throne is always a good idea. If you're a local band, don't ask the touring band to use their equipment. Bring all your gear, clothes, makeup, etc. and make sure you have everything you need for your performance.

STAGE PLOT / INPUT LIST AND RIDER

Stage plots/input lists are diagrams that explain what your stage setup consists of so the venue can be prepared. You can get as detailed as you want, it's just for the sound engineer to know what they're gonna be dealing with. A rider is the preferred catering for the green room.

STAGE PLOT
CONTACT INFO

INPUT LIST
1. Drums
2. Bass Amp
3. Guitar Amp
4. Vocal Mic

SOUNDCHECK VS. LINE CHECK

Soundchecks are usually reserved for the headliner, unless there's time before doors for more bands to soundcheck. This is when the band gets their monitor mixes, tests their instruments to make sure everything works and sounds good, test the lighting, effects, pyrotechnics, etc. The openers or support acts get *line checks*. Those are real quick plug in and go setups. The best thing to do for a line check is play a few extra bars in the beginning of the first song to give the sound guy time to make adjustments.

There's a good chance that the monitor mixes won't be how they were at soundcheck. Not sure why that happens but it always does. Don't be a diva. Be flexible and roll with it.

BE AWARE OF YOUR SURROUNDINGS

Don't play your instruments while someone is setting up mics in front of your drum kit or amp.

LEAVE THE IN-EARS AT HOME

If it's your first tour, make it easy on yourself and everyone else and try to get by without in-ears. Julia and I opened for a band once that almost *cancelled the show* because they didn't know how their giant rack of in-ears/backing tracks worked. That's inexcusable. You should be able to play under any condition, in-ear or no in-ear, click track or no click track, monitor or no monitor, you get the idea. After a few hours of troubleshooting, they figured out the volume was turned down and they didn't have to cancel the whole show.

THE GUEST LIST

I don't like to use the word hate, but I hate the guest list. It's a special kind of stress when someone asks me to put them on, then I forget because I'm busy with show stuff, then they show up, then there's no more spots because we're the opener or the list is full and I have to be that guy who bugs people to get someone into a show. Then there's the babysitting, the drink tickets, the doe-eyes about getting backstage, and so on… Please understand that the band pays for every person they put on the list. The guest list spot is not a way to support the band you love. Now even the mention of the guest list sends me into the blackest hole of despair that I still haven't fully emerged from. Is this worth not paying the $10 to get in? Is my lifelong misery worth feeling special for the five seconds it takes to see your name on **THE LIST?** It's not like you're getting in to some exclusive VIP bottle service fashion week party or something, it's just a show. At a bar.

One more thing about guest lists; if you ask to be on a guest list and don't show up, you're being very rude.

BUYOUTS

Buyouts are moneys you get for food, usually a crisp $20 bill each. In the US they don't treat you as good as they do in Europe where the shows are usually catered and the food kicks ass.

GET GOOD AT BEING... NOT SO GOOD

You're on stage playing and hit a wrong note. That used to be the kiss of death for me because I would instantly go into "shit shit shit don't fuck up again" mode which lasted for 5-10 minutes. Over time I learned to brush it off and keep playing like nothing happened. Nobody will ever know that you made a mistake, nor will they care. Practice brushing it off and it won't be a problem.

ADVICE FOR OPENING BANDS

Here's a few loving suggestions for how to make the opener a better experience for everyone.

• BE NICE! CREW ARE PEOPLE TOO

Venue staff, security and the people doing sound are on your team. They are allowing you to perform at their place and trying to help you succeed. Be cool with them. Sound guys are notorious for being grumpy. I never understood why until

I started doing live sound and became enlightened. Bigger bands are usually very nice, respectful and appreciative. New bands tend to think they're rockstars or whatever. The bands who were the rudest were the ones on their first tour, usually a three day don't-have-to-miss-work extravaganza. Some bands get insecure about their lack of performance skills and blame the monitor mixes, constantly saying turn me up or turn me down and publicly berating the sound engineer during their set. Don't do that.

• KNOW YOUR SET TIMES

Nothing worse than an opener who starts late and/or goes way over their time slot. This eats into the show/pushes back the set times and can burn the crowd out before the headliner goes on. Plus, it will most likely piss everyone off and make you all look like a bunch of amateurs.

• KEEP STAGE BANTER LIGHT

The only thing you should really say between songs is "thanks, we're so-and-so and this is our last song" and play one of the shorter ones. Don't say we have four more songs or three or even two. Banter exhausts people and so does waiting. Save the shtick for when you're a headliner. PS, starting your set by telling the audience to come closer to the stage just makes everyone uncomfortable. I'm not saying don't do it, I'm just saying it makes everybody in the venue very uncomfortable.

• DON'T REVEL IN IT

A reveler is a person or band who takes their sweet ass time breaking down their gear after a set, winding cables or having a post-set band celebration meeting on stage. Don't revel, wrap it up and get off the stage.

• CHILL!

This last tip is for everyone, headliner or opener who is second on the bill. After a band is done playing, don't charge the stage and start setting up before the previous band is done breaking down. You'll have your chance, just chill out.

BE EASY TO WORK WITH

If you're easy to work with, people will want to work with you. Show up on time and do what you say you're gonna do.

GREENROOM ETIQUETTE

The green room is the most important place in the whole world for the artist. The purpose of a green room is to give the artist a place away from the world so they can get in the right headspace to perform to the best of their ability. The only thing that matters in the life of a performer is the quality of the performance. Your pre-show mental condition should be protected like it's the most precious thing in your whole life. Think of a still pond in a misty forest, disturbance free. Even the smallest pebble can disrupt the serenity and affect the whole performance. Here's a few things that can really throw someone off before a show, in no specific order:

- Being stressed/rushed
- Guest list issues/guest list guilt
- A call from Mom
- Being locked in a conversation with a punisher
- Band member is missing
- Technical problems of any kind
- A call from Mom

Don't go in anyone else's green room unless you're invited in, and even then, don't touch people's food, drinks, back-packs, drugs, etc. and no matter what, never use their bathroom before the show. The bathroom is the heart of the green room. If you aren't kicked out with everyone 30 minutes before the show by a good tour manager, make sure you don't hog up the toilet before it's their time to be on stage. If there's only one green room, let the headliner have it and don't go in there. Most likely the headlining band is on tour which means they're exhausted and might not want a bunch of people invading their space. If you are sharing one green room, keep your stuff contained to one area and don't trash the place.

Don't put stickers on the mirrors, people need those.

DON'T BE A PUNISHER

A punisher is someone who wants to talk to you more than the average person would. They may trap you in a long ass conversation when you should be warming up for the show. They can fill your head with all kinds of terrible scenarios and unprovoked emotions. Punishers offer unsolicited advice and post-show critiques and often ask for elaborate favors. Punishers often start up conversations while you're in the middle of something like packing up and keep a conversation going way after the natural end point. If you're talking to a band member at the merch table, keep it short and don't block the table. Blocking the merch might make the band lose sales.

BANDS NEED SPACE

Don't talk to the band for at least thirty minutes before and ten minutes after they play. That means friends, family and other bands need to hold their horses before charging into the green room.

COVER YOUR GEAR IN THE VAN

Bands get robbed all the time. Buy a tarp and cover your gear any time you're not with it in the van. In the bay area, bring everything inside at night. Do NOT leave anything inside the vehicle in San Francisco overnight. If a hotel has valet parking, use it.

DON'T TAKE THE HEADLINER'S PARKING SPOT

That bus-size parking spot in front of the venue isn't meant for the opening bands. Park somewhere else.

TOUR VEHICLES

I don't recommend using an electric car to tour. There are a couple places to rent vehicles:

BANDAGO.COM

Bandago is a van rental specifically for bands.

TURO.COM

Turo is Airbnb for cars. If you can fit, get a minivan. See if there's one that takes E85 or *flex fuel.*

E85

This is 85% ethanol which means it cuts emissions down 85% and I've never seen it over $3/gallon. The MPG isn't as good as regular gas but whatever. There's an app called Pearson Fuels that tells you where the gas stations are that carry E85. Most cars can be modified to take E85 gas, it only costs around $50. Look into it if you're interested.

SAFETY AT SHOWS

Safety is the most important thing. Everyone needs to stay vigilant and look out for each other at shows. People can get too drunk/weird/violent. It's important to not be one of those people. Report problems to venue staff and security before things escalate. If you see something sketchy happening while you're playing, it's OK to stop a show to address it.

If you play music, at some point you're going to be around and/or offered drugs. Music and drugs are eternally bonded in music lore which gives a kind of false sense of casualness about their use. Regardless of your views on drugs, the fact is that they A. are very illegal and B. might be cut with fentanyl which will most likely kill you. Being a musician does not mean you're above the law or immune to overdosing. If anything, it increases your chances of getting busted and/or getting a bad batch.

Drug messaging is full of hypocrisy and double standards. Children are given amphetamines and melatonin, ketamine is used to treat depression, weed for cancer and lymphoma, cops have coke parties, big pharma lobbies politicians to push opiates, and don't even get me started on priests. It's total bullshit when anyone in the U.S. says, "don't do drugs". If anything, the person being lectured is going to have an inverse reaction (see TRENDS chapter) and do drugs!

Education is key for everything in life and drugs are no exception. Drugs can lead to addiction, health problems, loss of friends, family and job, but hitting rock bottom can easily be done without drugs too! Drugs and addiction are two separate subjects because you can be addicted to things that aren't drugs. Drug addiction and habitual drug use are different things as well. Regardless of the frequency or urgency of use, drugs can mess things up big time whether you're addicted or not. It's important to be educated about the choices you're making, and if you choose to partake then at the very least keep drug testing kits on hand to be sure you're consuming what you think you're consuming. It's also a good idea to keep some Narcan handy just in case.

Everyone has their process of growth and the introduction of drugs to anyone's life can be a major turning point. I'm not one to judge, everyone has their own life to live. I'm approaching this subject from a business perspective, which means that keeping your overhead low and being able to play shows is the top priority. Buying drugs in every city you visit will get pretty pricey and touring has a large overhead anyway. There's a lot of travel involved in music and every country has their own drug laws. Using band money to buy drugs is stupid for a lot of reasons.

Whatever you're gonna do, it's best if you keep things kosher while you're in public and on the road. Majority of a tour is spent driving, so it's best not to speed and best not to carry illegal substances with you, especially across state lines. If you're touring the US, there's a checkpoint outside of Juarez that has dogs and will search your van. Weed is illegal in most states and Texas is no exception. If you have a DUI, you can't get into Canada and if you've been arrested, Japan and Australia are hard to get into as well. In Germany they can pull you over and search you for no reason and drug test you right there on the side of the road and deport you or worse.

When crossing any border, best not lie because they're trained for that and they can see everything you've ever done in their records, even if it's been expunged. Other countries have super harsh drug laws that include life in prison and even the death penalty. If one person in the van has drugs on them, most likely everyone in that van is getting arrested. Even passing a joint is considered trafficking. People will bring drugs to try to get into your green room which can also cause problems. Use discretion about who you let in.

BAD HABITS

Imagine everything you ever want being thrown at you every night and having to avoid overindulgence. Bad habits start small, and it's very easy for them to become routine. You cheat on your girlfriend once, then you justify doing it again because hey you already did it so what's the big deal if it happens again. And again, and again. Any action can be justified, no matter how extreme or destructive. It's not until you take a step back, compare your new self to who you were before you broke your own rules and realize that you've completely lost who you used to be. Have fun and be safe but if you can't keep your shit together maybe you should re-evaluate your choices.

DON'T FEAR THE FEAR

If anyone who hasn't tried drugs is going to try drugs, you should be aware of a little thing called *coming down* otherwise known as THE FEAR. It's what happens when your chemicals get thrown outta whack and you go into a manic-depressive state. During this time, do NOT trust yourself or make ANY important decisions. If it feels like your entire life is crumbling, when it didn't feel like that yesterday, maybe you shouldn't trust yourself at that moment. Chill out, drink some water, have a sandwich and give your serotonin levels some time to replenish. Coming down on tour is bad, because you probably made some bad decisions the night before and you're coming down in a van with nothing to do but think about those decisions. True mental prison. Just remember, it's all gonna be ok. Relax and try to think about something else, or at least don't bug everyone else about it.

Don't start doing drugs too late in life. Usually, people start when they have no money and nothing to lose. Starting to experiment with drugs when you have money for more drugs is a horrible idea.

Euro speed is not the same as American speed. American speed is meth. I don't know what Euro speed is, but it's not meth.

Avoid any of those *one molecule away* drugs. If you're at a show or a club or a festival and someone offers you something and says yea it's legal because it's one molecule away from so-and-so, say no thanks and move on.

If you or someone in your band is looking for help with medical or drug treatment, reach out to MusiCares.org, a nonprofit organization affiliated with The Grammys. They may be able to help pay for it. More info about that in "The Grammys" chapter.

HE'S ABOUT TO LEARN THE MOST IMPORTANT LESSON IN THE MUSIC BUSINESS: DON'T TRUST PEOPLE IN THE MUSIC BUSINESS.
- HOMER SIMPSON

The slave trade, the Sackler family, Enron, Fox News. Though unpaid labor, drug addiction, lack of retirement and psychotic fanaticism over manufactured reality are common aspects of the music biz, I bring these up because their underlying theme: the willingness of human beings to exploit, lie, cheat, steal, pollute and destroy countless lives for money.

Music history is full of stories of the ambitious taking advantage of the naive. The winners will always be the ones who are playing the game vs. the ones that aren't, or at least not aware of it. Blackmail, extortion, false promises, it's all on the table. Be careful who you let into your organization because the more money there is to gain, the more extremes people will go to get it. There are predatory individuals and organizations that will infiltrate, destroy and absorb everything valuable you have, like an insect who injects digestive fluids into its victim and drinks a gutsmosa for brunch. This is a game that can take years and these parasites can be patient, making small almost unnoticeable moves, creating dissent among band members, slowly creeping into control of the money, accounting, contracts, and before you know it your guts have been sucked out. They can get lawyers on their side, accountants on their side, whatever it takes. Be aware of the nuances! *Don't ignore the warning signs*!

The way to combat this is to communicate! If you're leaving someone in charge of all the deals and money, check their work! Hire an accountant to double check that what these people are claiming is happening is actually happening and for fucks sake read the contracts yourself with a lawyer before signing anything. Do not give ANYONE authority to copy/paste your signature on any documents or contracts. Verify all copy/pasted signatures with the owners of those signatures.

There's a difference between illegal and actionable. When a law is broken you can call the cops for free, but when a contract is breached you call business cops (aka lawyers), which cost around $700/hour, give or take. Then you (at best) settle out of court or (at worst) litigate which can drag on for months or years and the costs can be astronomical. Lawyers generally don't take credit cards so he with the cash shall prevail. There is no good or bad in business, only broke or financially able to hire lawyers to drag out litigation and bleed out the opposing party dry until they finally cave. Either case, the lawyers are the real winners.

Financial gain isn't the only motivation for some upstanding individuals in society either, sometimes climbing the social ladder is currency enough. I bought a drum set from a dude who told me he was selling the kit to pay for lawyers because his band was blackmailing him. See, this band was pulling some underhanded shit for publicity that he didn't agree with. He was being threatened with false allegations of sexual misconduct if he went public with their scheme. Super dirty. Nobody should have to go through that. The crazy thing is that later that day he told me that they settled and signed an NDA so that was the last he could ever talk about it.

The part of this that really stings is the band will always have access to the money you helped make. If the band decides to stab you in the back and leave you for dead, you might not have the resources to fight back. Your work, your time and success can and will be used against you.

Sometimes you're put in a no-win situation and there's nothing you can do about it. You've been ambushed and the only lesson you learn is that people can be super shitty. The world is full of stories of injustice and regardless of what we all think should happen or might be fair, the person who is willing to stoop the lowest will usually come out on top. Situations change and sometimes life forces people to make tough choices. The band life is fun but it's also volatile, and if someone gets knocked up or arrested and needs money they can turn into a barely recognizable version of themselves.

People tend to trust their friends, and bands are usually groups of buddies that start a business. If you can sleep comfortably knowing you fucked over your friends, then the world is your oyster.

WOULD YOU OPEN A DELI WITH YOUR COKEHEAD FRIENDS?

OPERATING AGREEMENTS

News flash: bands break up. Like a divorce, this can take years and cost a lot of money. Operating agreements are like band prenups. If you're serious about the band and it has multiple members, bite the bullet and hire a lawyer to help sort one out. It's all fun and games until money gets involved and there wasn't a conversation about who gets what or where that money goes. Create a business plan and discuss money ***before*** you start making it. Having no plan is the recipe for disaster. Ideally everyone in the band should have their own lawyer.

SONG SPLITS

Song splits are the percentages of songwriting/publishing royalties paid to each contributor. When a song is written, if there's more than one writer, make sure you discuss and agree on the song splits. These should be consistent to your ASCAP/BMI, SoundExchange Direct and TheMLC accounts.

Make sure each contributor has their own account, not *the band* account. That's just stupid. Don't be stupid.

Don't use the band name as a replacement for member's names on the album credits. That would be like saying the U.S. Constitution was written by the USA. It makes no sense and helps nobody. You're not a band; you're a group of individuals and deserve credit for your work. Make sure you credit everyone for their contributions for writing, recording, art, etc. Get as detailed as you can because album credits are like a resume. Some people may want to continue working in the music business and if they don't have credits, they can't prove what they've accomplished. It would be like working for ten years and not being able to accurately list that on your job experience. Some bands get bitchy after a divorce and won't talk to past members. There's a chance you won't be able to add credits to albums once you realize you need them.

WHAT IS AN LLC

An LLC is a Limited Liability Corporation. It protects the band members from legal action but also binds the band members in a business contract. Some of the bigger festivals have auditors and requirements so make sure you have proper paperwork. Make sure to file tax returns if you open an LLC. Do your own research on this topic because each state and country has different rules and fees. Consult an accountant and a lawyer before making any big business decisions.

NEVER SIGN A CONTRACT WITHOUT THE HELP OF A LAWYER.

Business is the dark matter of music. It's the invisible glue that holds the art universe together. It operates beyond the boundaries of morality and cares not for the fate of humans or planets or galaxies. It's stronger than the darkest black hole and the brightest star. The source of business' power is the contract, a singular document that can be used to create and destroy, a power ignited by one mark, a signature, an X, inked in blood and bound for eternity.

Contracts can say all kinds of fun things. One word that you should be familiar with is *perpetuity* which means forever. For ever ever? FOR EVER EVER. One contract that I signed names the territory of the contract as "the universe". Meaning that this contract applies throughout the entire universe, so the only way out of it would be if I crossed over into a different dimension, depending on if you think all dimensions exist in the same universe. Now that particular contract I think is great, mutually beneficial and I enjoy working with the other parties involved. But if that contract was bad (meaning

I didn't read the fine print or understand completely what I was signing), it could potentially destroy everything I've ever worked for. Signing a contract is literally signing away your freedom to negotiate further.

BE CAREFUL WHO YOU ACCEPT MONEY FROM

An exchange of cash can be considered a deal. Before you accept money from anyone, do your due diligence on who that person is.

THERE'S NO SUCH THING AS A VERBAL CONTRACT. GET EVERYTHING IN WRITING.

Getting signed is the dream of every band. Someone believes in you enough to invest time and money into promoting your music. It's a confirmation that your efforts are starting to pay off and your hard work and talent is being recognized. This is a major turning point in the story of any band or artist. Whether that's a good turning point or a bad turning point depends on the label and the contract.

There are good labels and not so good labels out there. New bands usually don't have the skills to make the most informed decisions. There are plenty of stories where rights and royalties are signed away because of impulsive decision making, lack of experience, no leverage, big promises, etc. It's difficult to make major decisions when you're clueless about the possibilities and have no frame of reference for the ramifications of these choices.

Working with a label can be a fun and mutually beneficial relationship. Julia and I have both very much enjoyed collaborating with Everloving and Suicide Squeeze for the twenty plus years we've been working together. Just remember to READ THE CONTRACT and don't be afraid to turn down or modify offers you don't like. It's a red flag when one party won't listen to the other party's thoughts or concerns about a contract.

DEADLINES

Record contracts can require the artist to turn in multiple records on a specific release schedule. Now you have to juggle touring/writing/recording/making music videos/art/promotional materials/rehearsal. It's an enormous amount of work. If you're a perfectionist who wants to push yourself to make great music, this is your time to shine. The ancient Greeks had a word *aristeia* which means "moment of excellence in battle" and can end in the death of the warrior. It can feel like a battle when you are trying to create your best work on a deadline. Some have even turned to drugs to help boost their creativity, though I'm not sure that ever helps. The point is, always make the deadlines and do what you agreed to do.

WHAT IS AN ADVANCE?

A very misunderstood concept of being a signed musician is that money is free and when you get signed you get rich and it's party time. That's wrong wrong wrong. An advance is a loan. It's money given to an artist by a label that needs to be paid back, which is called *recouping*. If I get $20k to fund a record, I don't get paid album sale royalties by the label until that 20k gets recouped. Nothing is free, not even money.

IS A LABEL NECESSARY?

Being an unsigned band has its perks too! With the rise of distribution platforms like TuneCore and CD Baby, you have all the means necessary to get your music on all DSP's (Digital Service Providers) and keep all the money you earn from the streams on these platforms (royalties). Most likely you're going to start your music journey by self-publishing. This is the time to wrap your head around what's happening and gain a following, so you have some leverage and understanding about the business. Negotiation is all about leverage so go out and get some!

Managers can have a tremendous impact on a band's career. Their job has a wide range, which can include general strategy, handling the business, being the point of contact. It may even include artistic input on band branding, styling, songwriting and a band's sound. A good manager has connections, resources and great ideas to help a band live up to its fullest potential. Julia and I and grateful for the managers we've collaborated with over the years.

Managers are great to have, but there's a cost involved. Depending on the deal, managers can take a percentage of all the band's income streams: shows, merch, album sales, all of it. Don't worry about having a manager until you're at the level where it makes sense to hand responsibility and the extra 10-20% of all your earnings to someone else.

MISMANAGEMENT

Mismanagement is real. A bad manager can misuse their power and influence which can change a band dynamic for the worse. Some managers view artists as a product rather than a human (or group of humans). They can overwork you with no regard for your health or well-being and make bad deals on your behalf. They can steal your money, your royalties and your whole band if they're savvy!

A few short stories about famous managers:

THE BEATLES

Brian Epstein was a major contribution to the success of the Beatles, getting them into suits and cleaning up their image.

ELVIS

Colonel Tom (AKA Andreas Cornelis van Kuijk), wouldn't let Elvis leave the US to perform overseas because he (The Colonel) was in the country illegally and wouldn't be able to get back in if he left. He also used Elvis to pay off his 30 million in gambling debts to Vegas with zero regard for his safety or well-being.

NWA

Jerry Heller was accused of financial mismanagement.

THE BACKSTREET BOYS

Lou Pearlman went to prison for a Ponzi scheme.

JIMI HENDRIX

Michael Jeffrey has been accused of murdering Jimi for the insurance money by the roadie.

Booking Agents contact venues, book shows and work with management to route tours. Most likely, you won't start working with an agent right away. They want to work with a band or artist that wants to tour consistently and has a following. Since they work on commission, agents most likely aren't going to start working with you until you have a draw because there's not much money in small bands. Think about it, 10% of $100 is $10. That's not very much money, considering the amount of work it requires. Even $100/show is still not very much, and it takes years for a band to make more than $1,000/show. Start playing shows and let an agent come to you.

Booking shows is something you can do yourself, see the "Booking Shows" chapter.

BandsInTown is a great resource for venues and local bands to play with.
www.bandsintown.com

Out of all the jobs on this list, I think tour manager is the most challenging. Tour managers have an almost impossible job of making the tour work. For small bands they usually drive, sell merch, settle with the venue and keep things on track. A larger production has more moving parts like managing a crew, a driver, the band, communicating with venue staff, arranging flights and transportation, finding missing people, making sure the promoter doesn't steal the money while the band is on stage, dealing with the van breaking down, dealing with the bus breaking down, dealing with attitudes and dietary restrictions of everybody on tour, answering the same questions all the time and dealing with everybody's problems while staying calm and professional.

A tour itinerary will help keep everyone on the same page. Print out multiple copies and include show schedule, drive times, venue addresses, load-in and set times. Every tour is different and requires different planning.

Tour apps that can help keep everyone organized:
Master Tour by Eventric - www.eventric.com
Daysheets - www.daysheets.com

A publicist is a liaison between the artist and the media. They draft press releases about upcoming tours, music, etc., and use their extensive list of contacts to secure press coverage. They can also arrange appearances and interviews.

If you want to be your own publicist, put together a press release for any announcement. Make sure it's short, to the point, and fits on one sheet. Include a big bold headline, then a who, what, where, when, why and how, along with contact info, interview availability and a photo. Send this press release to any media outlet you feel is relevant.

Publicists can also be your PR (public relations) coach and can teach you the art of Media Training i.e. how to spin any questions back to a narrative you want to convey. Media training is a good skill to have. There's also a concept called *Crisis PR*, which can help you manage a bad situation (see the TROLLS chapter).

Paid ads on social media can spread the word as well but they can get pricey and their efficacy is debatable.

RADIO

Radio is an important part of music promotion and discovery. Check out www.radio.net or www.radio.garden for a list of global radio stations. Look for contact info on their websites and reach out directly.

Here's a sample press release for this book:

HOW TO BE SELF-RELIANT IN...
THE MUSIC BUSINESS

A NEW BOOK BY
JULIA KUGEL ★ SCOTT MONTOYA

Book preorder date 3/6/2026 · Release date 5/22/2026
Contact: howtobeselfreliantbook@gmail.com
howtobeselfreliant.com

Released in conjunction with the new Soft Palms record *In Echo, HOW TO BE SELF-RELIANT IN THE MUSIC BUSINESS* is a book about what we've learned during our lives in music. It's an essential read for DIY musicians and gives practical advice about the business, the lifestyle, etiquette, tour, recording, music royalties and much more.

Julia Kugel & Scott Montoya have been in music for over twenty years. They are married and live in Long Beach, CA. They release music / tour as Soft Palms and Julia, Julia.

Julia Kugel is founding member of the all-female punk band The Coathangers and has released solo records under White Woods and Julia Julia. Her latest album *Sugaring A Strawberry* was released 11/9/2024 on Suicide Squeeze Records.

Scott Montoya is a multi-instrumentalist / sound engineer / graphic designer / multimedia artist who spent ten years with psych band The Growlers.

Together they own and operate a nonprofit called Studios For Schools, an organization with the goal of providing recording equipment to underprivileged schools.

They organize a free community music "anti-music fest" in Long Beach called Happy Sundays. Their work centers around uplifting the community and helping future generations.

NO AI
NO AI WAS USED IN THE CREATION OF THIS BOOK

WEBSITE LINKS
SOFTPALMSMUSIC.COM
STUDIOSFORSCHOOLS.ORG
SCOTTWMONTOYA.COM
HEARJULIAJULIA.COM
HAPPYSUNDAYSFEST.COM

Nowadays, streaming is the primary way people consume music, but it's hasn't always been that way. First came vinyl records, then cassette tapes, then 8-tracks, then CDs, then downloads, now streaming. Streaming has made music more accessible (good), which depreciates its value (bad). Why pay for what you can get for free? Streamed music doesn't sound very good and generally doesn't pay very much to artists. Good for publicity, bad for everything else. Lots of artists are pulling their albums from streaming services for various reasons and they seem to be happy about their choice. The future of streaming is questionable because it doesn't put the artist first.

DOLBY ATMOS / APPLE SPATIAL AUDIO

Streaming services offer music in Dolby Atmos and Apple Spatial Audio. These formats aren't available on anything people can buy or own so there's no physical product artists can sell. Artists have an extra charge to get their records mastered or upmixed (converting a two-channel stereo mix to a 12-channel 7.1.4 Atmos mix). Downloading immersive albums isn't realistic because each track is about 700MB due to all the formats embedded in the file (a stereo track has two tracks and an Atmos ADM file contains up to 128 tracks of audio). Apple claims to pay 10% more to the artist when they submit their music in Spatial Audio but that's hard to verify. Immersive audio sounds good when you A/B it with the stereo mix, but whether it's worth the extra cost is up to you.

PLAYLISTS

Spotify might remove your music if you use paid playlist placement services. Don't do it. There are no for sure ways to get your music on playlists - fill out the form and hope that one of the music editors likes your song. All this talk about playlists and algorithms is totally beside the point, it's a way to get exposure but it's not the only way. Go play shows. Go on tour and sell merch. A $30 record is worth 10,000 streams.

Streaming doesn't pay artists enough money, but you get 0% of the money you don't collect. There's a step-by-step guide on registering for your royalites in the next chapter. As of 1/10/2026, the average rates per stream are:

SiriusXM	$44
Tidal	$0.01
Apple Music	$0.008
Amazon Music	$0.004
Spotify	$0.003
YouTube Music	$0.002
Pandora	$0.001
Deezer	$0.006

SOMEBODY START A NONPROFIT STREAMING SERVICE

I think it's worth taking a page to pitch an idea to the world:

The business model of a DSP relies on the exploitation of artists. Giving your money and time to a streaming service does not support artists, it only supports the streaming service. The income gap between the CEOs of these corporations and the artists that provide their product is appalling. A nonprofit does not have to answer to investors or board members whose main motivation is the bottom line. Take capitalist greed out of the equation and you'll have a win-win for artists and music lovers. An alternative that pays artists fairly, provides high quality audio and does not fund AI military research would be welcomed by all.

Thank you for your time.

Imagine getting a job where you don't know how much you're getting paid, and your money is split up and buried somewhere in the world in locked boxes and the key is an algebra equation. Music royalties are complicated. Some would say overly complicated on purpose, but that conspiracy theory is just ridiculous because who would want to be responsible for holding vast sums of squeaky-clean cash? Not an organization that most musicians find by accident, if they ever find it at all. There are companies that know where your money's buried and the maths to unlock it, but they take a cut.

Royalties are the monies paid when a song is sold, streamed, downloaded, played live, etc. There are a few types of royalties that are owed to rightsholders (songwriters, publishers, performers, labels, artists, etc.). This chapter gives a basic understanding of terms you need to know, and a step-by-step guide for new and existing artists to register and verify their works are properly registered. Each musician has a unique situation and song splits to consider.

COLLECTION SOCIETIES

Collection societies collect money from various sources on your behalf, and registering with them is the only way to access that money. They take a cut but there's no way around that. You don't have to be a citizen of the country these societies are based in to become a member. You can only be a member of one PRO but can be a member of multiple MRO's and CMO's. Just make sure they are all collecting from different areas and there's no overlap, or else that can lead to delays in payment.

• PRO - PERFORMING RIGHTS ORGANIZATION

PRO's collect performance royalties. In this context, performance means the use of your music in a retail or commercial space, which they issue licenses for. Think of it as a rental fee for your music.
ASCAP, BMI, SESAC*, GMR* are PRO's. *Invite only

• MRO - MECHANICAL RIGHTS ORGANIZATION

MRO's collect mechanical rights royalties, which is a fee for every time a copy of music is made, paid to the copyright owner(s). A stream/download is considered a copy.
TheMLC collects mechanical royalties in the US only. A CMO like SACEM can collect the rest, or you can sign up for multiple MRO's like CMRRA (Canada), MCPS (UK).

• CMO - COLLECTIVE MANAGEMENT ORGANIZATION

These collect both performance and mechanical rights royalties. PRO+MRO=CMO. SACEM (France) and GEMA (Germany) are both CMO's. TheMLC has a list of global CMO's here: www.themlc.com/cmo-members

• NRO - NEIGHBORING RIGHTS ORGANIZATION

NRO's collect royalties for the performers on the recordings and the copyright holders of the songs. SoundExchange is an NRO. They collect digital performance royalties from worldwide NRO's. SoundExchange Direct is the portal where artists and labels manage their catalogs on SoundExchange.

• RECORD LABELS & DIGITAL DISTRIBUTORS
These collect from the music distributors or DSP's that carry the product (recordings).

TYPES OF ROYALTIES AND WHO COLLECTS THEM

There's a difference between a song (composition) and the recording of a song. Both can have different owners and royalty splits. Royalties are collected from different sources for copyright ownership, songwriting, performance, sales of physical product and mechanical licensing of the music.

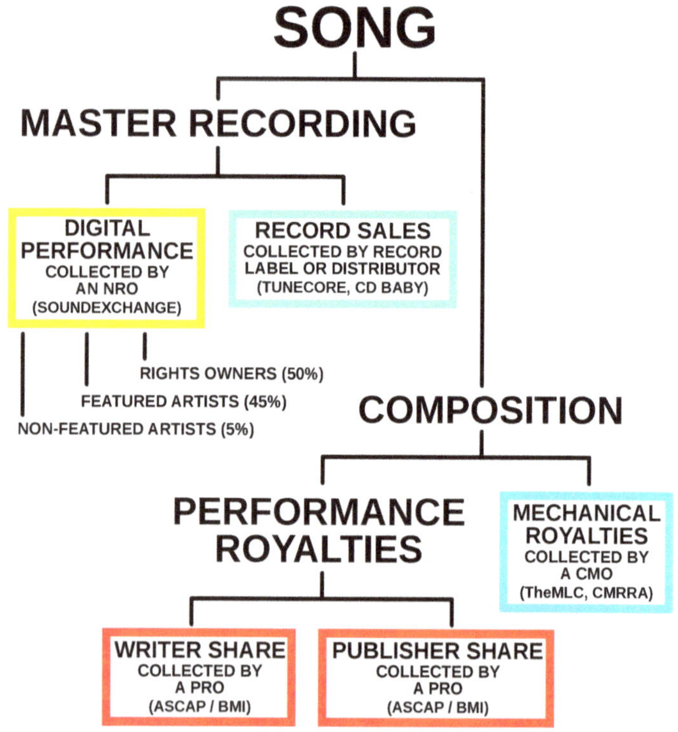

ASCAP / BMI (PRO)

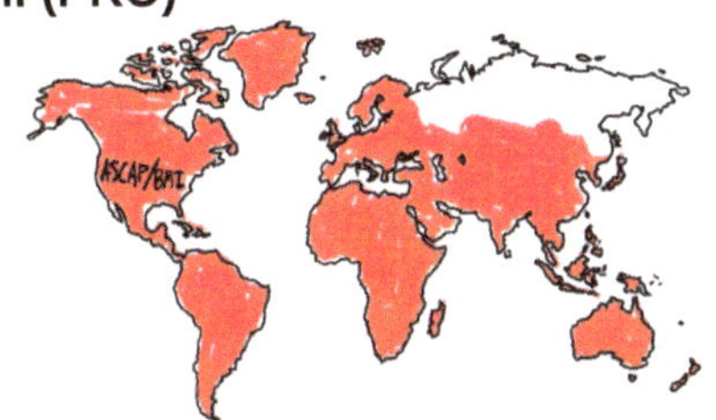

TheMLC (MRO) & SACEM (CMO)

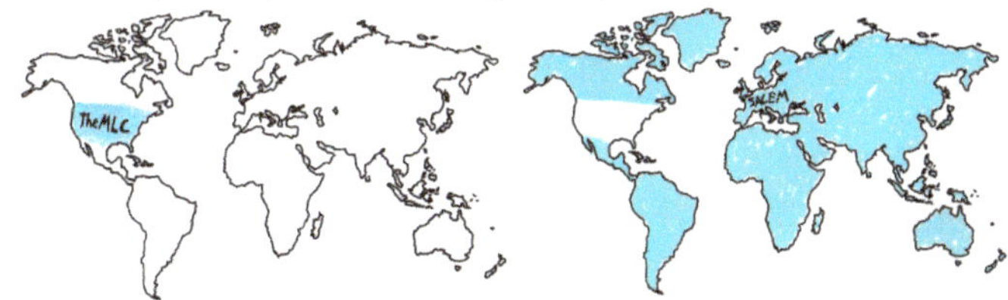

SOUNDEXCHANGE (NRO)

RECORD LABELS & DIGITAL DISTRIBUTORS

AFM SAG-AFTRA
(NON-FEATURED ARTISTS VIA IPRD FUND)

If you've ever had music on a TV show or a movie, search your name on their site. If you have unclaimed royalites, your name will come up. If nothing appears, you don't have any. The link is below, or search AFM SAG-AFTRA Unclaimed.
www.afmsagaftrafund.org/Search/Unclaimed

TERMS TO KNOW

SONGWRITER

Writer of a song (composition).

PUBLISHER

A publisher publishes a written song. Think of a publisher as an agent of a songwriter. You are your own publisher unless you are working with a publishing administrator. At some point, the powers that be realized that publishers were ripping off the songwriters they represent, so they mandated that fifty percent of publishing royalties go direct to the songwriter, and fifty percent go to the publisher. If you're self-published, you get 100% of those royalties.

DSP - DIGITAL SERVICE PROVIDER
(STREAMING SERVICE)

Amazon Music, Apple Music, Deezer, Pandora, Qobuz, Spotify, Tidal, YouTube Music

SONG CODES

ISRC–INTERNATIONAL STANDARD RECORDING CODE

ID given to a *recording.*

ISWC–INTERNATIONAL STANDARD MUSIC WORK CODE

ID given to a *work/composition.*

The ISRC is the code that represents the recording, and ISWC represents the composition. If I write and record a song, then record a live version of that song, those recordings will have different ISRCs but the same ISWCs. ISWCs always start with the letter T.

BOWI – BEST OPEN WORKS IDENTIFIER

Another work ID. I've never seen any other mention of a BOWI code outside of the music database site called Quansic which I highly recommend exploring (it's free).
www.explorer.quansic.com

PUBLISHING ADMINISTRATORS

There are companies who will collect publishing royalties on your behalf called Publishing Administrators. They collect publishing royalties from most of the world and take 15-20% of all the royalties they collect, on top of membership fees.
Kobalt, SongTrust, CD Baby Pro Publishing, TuneCore Publishing

TIP: Publishing administrators require that your royalties from TheMLC get funneled through them. If you have a back catalog and are thinking about joining a publishing administrator, sign up for TheMLC first, get the initial backlogged chunk of change and then sign up for the publishing administrator to collect everything moving forward.

ARTIST ID CODES

Knowing your codes and ID numbers helps with more accurate reporting and distribution by the whole chain.

ISNI – INTERNATIONAL STANDARD NAME IDENTIFIER

ISNI codes generally apply to credits for songs rather than

royalties. Each member of a band AND the band should have their own ISNI. For example, I have my own ISNI, Julia has her own ISNI, and Soft Palms has its own ISNI.

To see if you have an ISNI, search the database at www.isni.org/page/search-database/.

You should also search your own name using the free Quansic database at explorer.quansic.com.

If you don't have an ISNI, you can get one for free through Veva Collect. Veva Collect is a free music collaboration app where you can keep tracks of credits and get a free ISNI, very useful.
www.vevacollect.com

IPI – INTERESTED PARTY INFORMATION

This number is assigned to you when you sign up with a CMO, MRO or PRO. If you have aliases, those will each have their own IPI and will be connected to the same account.

IPN - INTERNTIONAL PERFORMER NUMBER

Another musician identifier similar to an IPI.

HOW TO REGISTER

Songwriters are responsible for registering their portion of a composition with their own PRO. For example, if Writer A is on ASCAP and Writer B on BMI, each writer must register independently with their own PRO to get their royalty shares. Once both parties have registered, ASCAP and/or BMI will create an ISWC for the track, but only after 100% of the splits are accounted for. Make sure you coordinate your efforts when registering. The two companies share a public database called

SongView, where they get info on the tracks like ASCAP and BMI work ID's and the ISWC's.

Here's a step-by-step guide on how to register and keep track of your music:

I. CREATE A DISCOGRAPHY SPREADSHEET

This can be done on a spreadsheet program like Google Sheets or Microsoft Excel. Make columns with Artist, Album Title, Track Title, Track Number, ISRC, ISWC, Song Split %, Release Date, ASCAP Work ID, BMI Work ID, MLC Song Code. Fill that sheet in! Other things to know are BPM, Key, Catalog Number, Label, Credits, Descriptors, anything else about the track you can possibly think of. I organize mine by album and track number, with the albums color-coded.

Artist	Album Title	Track Title	Track Number	ISRC	ISWC	Release Date
Artist 1	Album 1	Track 1	1	123456789001	T567298522	01/22/2021
Artist 1	Album 1	Track 2	2	123456789002	T567298534	01/22/2021
Artist 1	Album 1	Track 3	3	123456789003	T567298583	01/22/2021
Artist 1	Album 1	Track 4	4	123456789004	T567298587	01/22/2021
Artist 1	Album 1	Track 5	5	123456789005	T567298584	01/22/2021
Artist 1	Album 1	Track 6	6	123456789006	T567298588	01/22/2021
Artist 1	Album 1	Track 7	7	123456789007	T567298595	01/22/2021
Artist 2	Album 2	Track 1	1	98765432301	T123456717	04/20/2025
Artist 2	Album 2	Track 2	2	98765432302	T123456725	04/20/2025
Artist 2	Album 2	Track 3	3	98765432303	T123456745	04/20/2025

II. REGISTER FOR ASCAP OR BMI

1. If you don't have one, create an ASCAP or BMI account (not both). Pick one and search for *Free ASCAP writer and publisher* or *Free BMI account*.

- If you join ASCAP, create a writer account AND a publisher account.
- BMI collects writing and publishing royalties with one account. They use 200% to represent this.

• IPI's will be given to you right away, make sure you copy/paste those on your discography spreadsheet. ASCAP will give you two IPI's, one for your writer account and one for your publisher account.

2. If you already have these accounts, double check your works list to see if anything is missing and the percentages are correct.

3. Register your tracks. If you are registering a track that has both ASCAP and BMI members, enter your percentage and use *writer unknown* for the remainder. The other parties will have to register with their own PRO. Again, there won't be an ISWC code created for the track without 100% of the splits accounted for. This may cause problems when registering for TheMLC and SoundExchange and lead to incomplete or inaccurate reporting. Coordinate your efforts! It takes a few days to get an ISWC after registering with ASCAP/BMI.

EXAMPLE: Writer A is an ASCAP member and writer B is a BMI member. Writer A should register the track and put their percentage, and the remainder as *writer unknown* and *publisher unknown* for the percentages that are not theirs. Writer B should register the same track with BMI and enter *writer unknown* and *publisher unknown*. An ISWC code will be issued for the work once both Writer A and Writer B have registered their shares and 100% of the publishing is registered. An ISWC code will show up on the work's page in the ASCAP and BMI catalog in a few days. Wait times vary.

• Find your track's ISWC:
For ASCAP, check the *Performers & Other Info* on the work's page. For BMI the ISWC will be on the work's page.

• ASCAP and BMI have areas on their websites called *ASCAP OnStage* and *BMI Live*, where you can submit a claim for each time you perform your music live. Music venues pay a blanket license for all music being played in their establishment.

III. REGISTER FOR TheMLC

1. Sign up for a free account at TheMLC.com using your ISNI and IPI number (For ASCAP members, use your publishing IPI. For BMI, use either your writer or publisher IPI). It takes a couple days to verify your account.

2. Once you get verified, create a member profile.

3. Follow the directions on this page to register your work: www.help.themlc.com/en/support/how-to-register-works-in-the-mlc-portal

IV. REGISTER FOR SOUNDEXCHANGE DIRECT

SoundExchange Direct is the most confusing one. Take it slow, and if you get lost they have links to video tutorials for each step on the corresponding pages. If you've released music on a record label, communicate with your label to see if they have uploaded your tracks to SoundExchange. If you've self-released, you're most likely going to have to upload mp3s or WAVs of your music to register. Make sure the metadata (ISRC's artist name, track title) is embedded before uploading. More on metadata in the "Metadata" chapter.

1. Visit www.register.soundexchange.com to register for a free account.
2. If you're starting fresh, to go *My Catalog > Submit Recordings* and start adding recordings. Make sure you have the track's ISRC codes and other metadata embedded in the

audio files before you upload them. Enter as much info as you can on the Recording Entry page for each track (all this info should be stored on your discography spreadsheet). If you're confused, they have links to videos on how to do this.

3. Check to see if your tracks are already submitted to SoundExchange. Go to *My Catalog > Search & Claim* to start searching and claiming. Best to search using an ISRC code, but you can search by artist and song title too. *Claim as an Artist* if you performed on a track and *Claim as an RO* (Rights Owner) if you own the masters.

You will need to know what percentage of the song you have ownership of and claim that accordingly.

Note: Every performer on a song should be represented on the *Claim as an Artist* section of SoundExchange. Everyone in the band should have their own SoundExchange Direct account.

4. To allow SoundExchange to collect your worldwide royalties, go to your dashboard, click on your registrant account, and on the secondary menu click *More*, then on the dropdown menu click *Membership Summary*. Under *Mandate Territories*, make sure it says *Worldwide*. If it doesn't, click *Update* to the left and update it on the next screen.

• SoundExchange gives 5 percent of the royalties they collect to the AFM SAG-AFTRA (American Federation of Musicians & Screen Actors Guild American Federation of Television & Radio Artists) fund for *non-featured artists* (session musicians). They don't collect for every track, only the top

100 SoundScan recordings on the AHRA (Audio Home Recording Act) list, and the top 25,000 sound recording titles from the DPRA (Digital Performance Right in Sound Recordings Digital Millenium Copyright Act) list. These are the big tracks, or tracks on TV or movies only. To see if any of your tracks are on this list, go to www.afmsagaftrafund.org/ and explore the *Unclaimed Royalties* and the *Covered Royalties* pages.

COPYRIGHTING YOUR WORK

Your work is technically *yours* once you create it but if you want the ability to challenge someone who steals it, you have to register your work with the US Copyright office. The fee is $65 for published albums, $65 for individual tracks and $85 for unpublished albums. Just do it.
www.copyright.gov/registration

THE BLACK BOX

Somehow a term came into being that makes people think there's a large sum of money in a black box somewhere. If you have been making music for a long time and haven't been collecting your royalties, then yes, your money is most likely still there because nobody else can legally collect it for you. Follow the registration instructions earlier in this chapter to get your money.

COMEDY, SPOKEN WORD AND PODCASTS

Non-musical works do not generate the same royalties as musical works because they are not represented by organizations that issue music licenses (ASCAP/BMI, TheMLC).

Two organizations that collect for non-musical works are:

SOUNDEXCHANGE

www.soundexchange.com
SoundExchange "...collects royalties for ALL sound recordings played on non-interactive digital radio. This includes recordings and soundtracks made by actors, comedians, and spoken word artists in addition to musicians". - soundexchange.com
Tell any comedian, poet or spoken word artist friends of yours to sign up for SoundExchange Direct.

SPOKEN GIANTS

www.spokengiants.com
According to Spoken Giants, they are the "first global rights administration company for the owners and creators of Spoken Word copyrights". They represent comedy, speeches, public readings and podcasts.

WHO GETS MY ROYALTIES WHEN I DIE?

Create a will and include your royalties in it. A *posthumous membership* can be created for a friend or loved one who never registered their music. Call the PRO/CMO/NRO for info.

Royalties confuse everyone, so don't get discouraged if it doesn't click right away. If you're researching further, go straight to the source. TheMLC has a great way of explaining the process on their site, and you can call TheMLC, ASCAP, BMI and SoundExchange Direct with questions, they're very helpful. I recommend avoiding publishing administrators' websites for your research because the information on those sites is a nebulous on purpose. Remember, they are trying to sell you a service. Straightening out your royalties takes a few months to complete so be patient. Don't let it fall through the cracks!

Creating content for social media is a bottomless pit of time and energy. Having a basic understanding of photo editing/ vector graphic/video editing software can really come in handy when creating show/tour posters, album art, shirt designs, music videos and other content in its various aspect ratios that fit on your Instagram, Facebook, TikTok, X, Bluesky, Mastodon, BandsInTown, Bandcamp, YouTube, LinkedIn, Spotify, Apple Music, Amazon Music, Deezer, Tidal and blog on your band website (which you should have for SEO purposes). Photoshop, Illustrator and InDesign are nice, but pricey. There are free alternative versions of the software so depending on your budget you might want to give those a shot.

For video, I really like the free version of DaVinci Resolve by Blackmagic design. In my experience it works faster and uses less processing power than Adobe Premiere, though I do like Premiere as well.

In Illustrator and InDesign, you can *place* files (link Photoshop & Illustrator files, images, pdfs, jpegs, pngs, etc.) on multiple artboards in the same file. This saves hard drive space because instead of having twenty images, you have one

image twenty times and if you make a change to that image, it changes them all automatically. I created a template that has the aspect ratios for every image size I could possibly need it for so it's easy to make every version of a tour poster containing the same image with different dates. I'm sure there's a way to do this quicker using AI but I don't care.
Don't use AI to make your show posters.

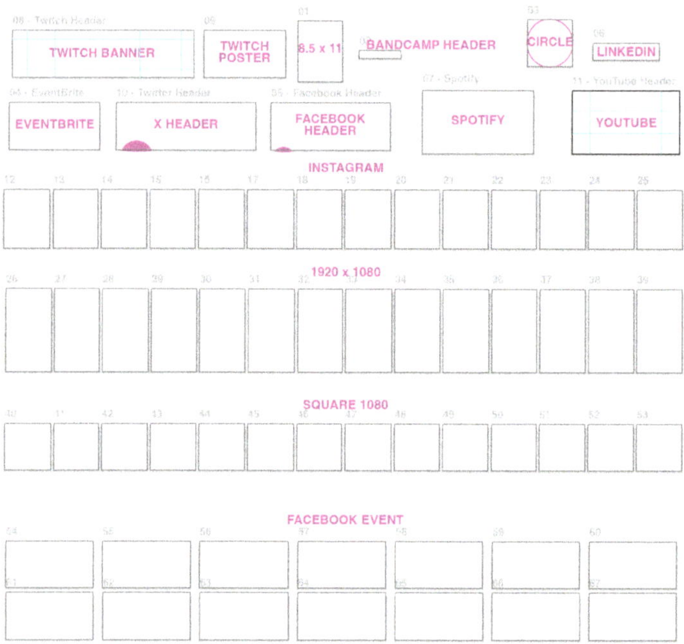

Campaign template for Adobe Illustrator
Download for free at howtobeselfreliant.com

Search Engine Optimization is the best way to create a presence online. It helps give search engine bots context and get your name higher up on search results making you look more legit. By learning these skills you'll be able to save thousands of dollars on proper SEO. I suggest buying carpal tunnel braces and blue blocker glasses to prevent injuries and pace yourself so you don't get overwhelmed. It's a lot to learn but eventually gets kinda fun.

WEBSITES THAT SEARCH BOTS TAKE SERIOUSLY

All these websites are data centers that search engine bots crawl, ingest and regurgitate. Entering in as much info on each site as possible will ensure you have proper credits and your discography is complete. SoundExchange also uses these sites to verify royalties. There's a learning curve on how to enter this information on each site so take your time.

ALLMUSIC.COM

Music database. You can submit changes, but I'm not sure who makes them or in what time frame.

DISCOGS.COM

Community-powered music database. Get as detailed as you can on your album notes because the Discogs community references those notes for the database.

MUSICBRAINZ.ORG

Community-powered music database.

WIKIDATA.ORG

Knowledge base, it's the center hub of the internet. This is where you should connect as many dots as you can.

WIKIMEDIA COMMONS

A site to upload photos. This is Google's first stop for images. Keep in mind anything uploaded here becomes public domain. If you want to have more control over the pictures that appear when you or your band is searched, upload them to Wikimedia Commons.

WIKIPEDIA.ORG

Community-powered encyclopedia.

TIP: When you get a write-up in a music blog, ask the author to put a link to your website on the article and make sure *no-follow* is unticked. This will allow search engine bots to crawl from the article to your website and ingest the information.

SHOW LISTING SITES

BANDSINTOWN.COM

Great, free, and can embed your calendar on your website. It also creates a show schema, though I wish I could edit the show schemas to give them more info.

SONGKICK.COM

Another free site for listing show dates. These dates are automatically updated on your Bandcamp website.

SCHEMAS

Schemas (Structured Data) are sets of tags embedded in the headers of websites that give search engine bots a better understanding of what the website is about. For instance, softpalmsmusic.com has a schema for the band that has member names, links to socials, album titles with track lists and all relevant info that I could think of. For tags like members, it has a references to other schemas @Julia-Kugel, which tells all about her, including a schema tag that references @ The-Coathangers and @Julia-Julia, which both have references to schemas about the band members, album schemas, track schemas, ISRC code schemas, label schemas, and so on. You're building a web of context to help search engines understand the world they will one day take dominion over.

SCHEMA RESOURCES

SCHEMA.ORG

Schema.org is a website that you can explore to get more information and test your schemas for errors.

SCHEMANTRA.COM

A genius website that has a schema generator and is a huge help when trying to wrap your head around schemas.

GOOGLE TAG MANAGER (GTM)

A fast way to embed/edit/keep track of schemas on your site. It can't embed the same tag on multiple sites so create a workspace (container) for each website.

GOOGLE SEARCH CONSOLE (GSC)

A service/dashboard where you can monitor your presence on Google. It has a graph with *impressions* and *clicks* that shows your progress and lets you know if any of your schemas are invalid.

SCHEMA EXAMPLE:

```
<script type="application/ld+json" class="schemantra.com">{
  "@context": "www.schema.org",
  "@type": "MusicGroup",
  "@id": "Soft-Palms",
  "description": "Music Project of Julia Kugel (The Coathangers, Julia Julia, Animal Self, Julia & The Squeezettes) & Scott Montoya (former member of The Growlers).",
  "location": "Long Beach, CA",
  "album": [
  {
   "@type": "MusicAlbum",
   "name": "Soft Palms",
   "@id": "Soft-Palms-Self-Titled"
  },
  {
   "@type": "MusicAlbum",
   "name": "In Echo",
   "@id": "In-Echo"
  }
  ],
  "name": "Soft Palms",
  "sameAs": [
   "www.facebook.com/softpalmsmusic/",
   "www.instagram.com/softpalmsmusic/",
   "www.x.com/softpalmsmusic",
   "www.bandsintown.com/a/14133446-soft-palms",
   "www.youtube.com/@softpalmsmusic",
  ],
  "url": "www.softpalmsmusic.com/",
   "member": [
    {
     "@type": "OrganizationRole",
     "member": {
      "@type": "Person",
      "@id": "Julia-Kugel"
     }
    },
    {
     "@type": "OrganizationRole",
     "member": {
      "@type": "Person",
      "@id": "Scott-Montoya"
     }
    }
   ]
 }

 }</script>
```

Music has a few types of metadata, some embedded in the audio, and some accompanies the audio on a separate file. This can include subjects such as artist, album name, artist name, track title and number, release date, label, ISRC code, etc. Different audio file types can contain different types of metadata, which is embedded to tracks during mastering. Digital distribution services embed metadata to tracks after they're uploaded too. It's important to have as much metadata embedded in your file as possible. If you get your mastered tracks back and they're blank, or you want to check them and add more, there are a couple desktop apps you can use to accomplish that. Drag the tracks in and enter the metadata manually.

MAC
META: Music Tag Editor from NightBirdsResolve
www.nightbirdsevolve.com/meta

WINDOWS & MAC
BWFMetaEdit
www.mediaarea.net/BWFMetaEdit

Mp3tag
https://www.mp3tag.de/

MUSIXMATCH
To make sure your lyrics are correct and sync'd up on streaming platforms, check out Musixmatch.
www.musixmatch.com

DDEX
DDEX is an organization that standardizes metadata to make the exchange of data and information across the music industry more efficient. This is not something that can be created by the regular person, but Session Studio and Veva Collect give you the ability to export .rin files which use the DDEX standard (it's an XML sheet). Submit those with your masters. If you want to learn more about DDEX, visit ddex.net.

Trip out on this: if you listen to any record that has never been digitized (not converted waveforms into 1's and 0's on a computer) you're hearing and feeling an *analog* (direct representation) of the energy that was created during that performance. Sound is acoustic energy which is captured by a microphone. Microphones are *transducers* (a device that converts one form of energy into another) which converts acoustic energy into very small voltages of electrical energy which is amplified through tubes, transistors or transformers. These are sent to magnetic heads on a tape machine which convert that electricity to fluctuating magnetic fields, aligning the metallic dust on the tape in such a way that when played back, the heads read these magnetic fluctuations, convert them back to electricity and vibrate speakers which push air to create sound waves. Your ears convert the vibrations into electrical energy, which is sent to your brain to interpret, and the mixtures of these various noises form some sort of emotional response which is what makes music so special. Major chords are happy, minor chords are sad, but why? Music is a form of emotional manipulation because it relies on the subconscious reactions we are all programmed with. It's a conversation we're having with billions of years of evolution. The choices made during the production of a record shouldn't necessarily be what sounds "good", but what best aligns with the way you're trying to trick the brain into reacting the way you want it to react. With different equipment you can fine tune this experience.

Photography is the art of capturing light; recording is the art of capturing sound. Electrons speeding through heated vacuum tubes (valves) and the magic of transformers can add aesthetic to a song, turning something that's already good into a sublime experience. Music is cool, but recording is cooler. Stylizing a recording is the same as stylizing clothing or a band logo or album art. *Sound Engineer* is a pretty stale name, considering the influence they give to the aesthetic of a record. *Sound Designer* is already a thing, they create sounds like footsteps and laser gun noises in movies/tv shows/video games, etc. *Sound Stylist* is more accurate, though I'm not sure anyone would adopt that.

Some bands are more phonogenic than others. When I was doing live sound, I experienced all kinds of bands. Some bands I couldn't make sound good no matter what I tried. Some bands all I had to do was turn up the faders (which is kinda sorta what a live sound engineer should only kinda sorta have to do, but that's a different conversation). Those bands have a supernatural quality about them, the combination of auras and energies between the performers that results in something greater than the sum of its parts. It's not just the instruments being amplified, it's the personalities of the players being projected out as well. Those personalities are formed by the experiences and genetics of an entire lifetime or multiple lifetimes and just so happen to mesh well (or not so well) with the other personalities in the mix. For this reason, when bands change members, it changes the experience. It's almost impossible to replicate chemistry between players.

Recording music is one of the most abstract artforms because you can't see or touch or taste anything you create. You are constructing an experience that relies on the listener's subconscious reactions to sound. Like any artform, getting an internship at a studio will give you information and knowledge that you'd otherwise be missing out on.

VINTAGE = BROKEN

Recording is fun *when everything works*. Vintage gear sounds good but don't fall into that trap too early on because you will probably buy something that doesn't work or doesn't work correctly. Tape machines are great when they work and if you're trying to learn how to fix/bias/align them then have at it. If you're trying to get the show on the road then stick with digital. Remember: vintage = BROKEN. There are better uses for your time and money than dealing with broken equipment (unless you plan on getting into audio electronics in which case hell yea). Don't get caught up in the trap of feeling like you must have the best mic or vintage preamps or whatever. The best microphone is the one in your hand. All that really matters is a great performance of a great song. Try to avoid having your flow interrupted as much as you can. Buy stuff that works and start developing your skills. Use each record as a learning experience for the next one.

MIXING TIPS

• Mixing level - Put a pink noise generator on the master output at -18 and turn the speakers to about as loud as a human voice talking. Mix at that level. Mark the speaker volume in case if you change it.

• Spend the extra time to make things sound good on the way IN. It's way easier to cook when the ingredients taste good.

• Let records grow into their own sound. There's always a struggle between what things sound like in your head and what you can achieve with the equipment you're working with. Every engineer has their own style, taste, room setup, mics, etc. All these variables are what make recording such a great and challenging art form.

• There's an audio repair program called iZotope RX. Clean up the tracks with RX before you start mixing. For drums and transient instruments, normalize the peaks to -6 and for non-transient instruments like guitar and vocals, normalize the integrated loudness to -24. Use volume automation to level out vocals and manage peaks. This will give you a great starting point on your mix. (Thanks Mick!)

• I always keep a previous mix of the track on the bottom of my mix session for a reference. This is a great way to see if I'm making things better or worse.

• Trust your meters! Mixing can be like flying a plane through clouds with no visibility. VU meters will tell you if you're too loud, a phase meter will tell you if you're out of phase. iZotope has a great plugin called Tonal Balance Control which will show you how the frequency content of your mix compares to those of similar styles of music.

HEADPHONE MIXES

Great performances come from great headphone mixes. Musicians play better when they sound good and hear themselves well. Spend the extra time to get good headphone mixes. Make them feel pretty.

TRANSFORMERS

My favorite electrical component is the transformer. They consist of a core with two or more coils wrapped around poles of the core. These windings create a magnetic field that generates current in the other coil. In audio, these magnetic fields cause a metamorphosis of sound. Different mixtures of metals create different characteristics in the audio, and this change depends on the mixture of iron/steel/nickel that make up the coils. Transformers are passive, which means they don't require power to operate, the source of their power is physics and the magic of the universe.

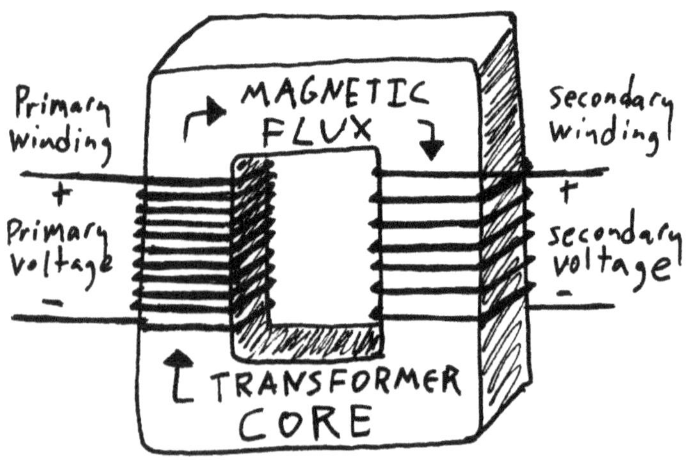

MASTERING

Mastering is the process of putting finishing touches on tracks and preparing them for delivery in various formats. It can be like varnish on a piece of wood, making it nice and smooth and shiny. I've never used AI for mastering and I don't recommend it. The mastering engineer should embed the track metadata on the masters. To help this process, put this list together send it along with the tracks:

MASTERING CHECKLIST

Artist name, album name, album year, copyright info, label name, track list, ISRC codes (if you have them), names of musicians, lyrics, cover art, studio name & engineer/assistant engineer, band website, label website, release date (if you know it).

MAKING YOUR OWN CABLES

Studio gear is expensive and takes a lot of cable. You can cut your cost way down and the quality way up by making your own! All it takes is a soldering iron and time. The cable also comes in every color of the rainbow you can pair with colored heat shrink for when you feel festive. You can make 3-pin XLR, 5-pin XLR, 8-pin XLR, ¼" (instrument) cables, DB25, patchbays, headphone extenders, RCA cables easily. Eventually you'll graduate to repairing your own guitars, microphones, and who knows maybe you'll even have a career in audio electronics. Cabling and tips can be bought PacRad.com, SweetWater.com, Markertek.com, Redco.com and most electronic supply stores carry this stuff too.

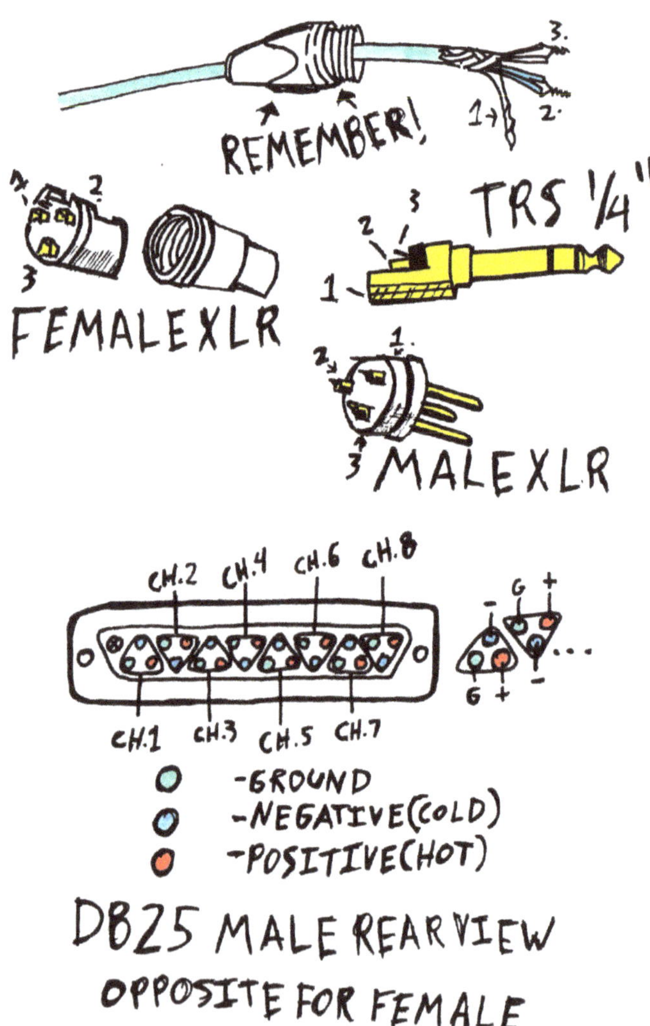
3.
REMEMBER!
1
2.
1
2
3
FEMALE XLR
TRS 1/4"
3
2
1
1.
2
3
MALE XLR
CH.2
CH.4
CH.6
CH.8
G
+
-
-
G
+
CH.1
CH.3
CH.5
CH.7
-GROUND
-NEGATIVE (COLD)
-POSITIVE (HOT)
DB25 MALE REARVIEW
OPPOSITE FOR FEMALE

HOW TO BUILD CABLES

I. Prep your raw cable. This is using Canare L-4E6S Star-Quad cable.

1. Strip 1/2 inch of insulating layer off the ends of the cable.
2. Unbraid the shielding and twist into one strand. This will be the ground.
3. Strip the ends of the white wires and twist the copper together, same with the blue wires. Melt some solder on the loose copper to hold it in place.

II. Solder to the tips! See illustrations on previous page. Remember to put the twist-on part on the cable before you start soldering or else you'll have to unsolder everything and start over.

XLR

Look on the XLR tip bodies, those have a 1,2 and 3 on the terminals.

- 1 - Ground
- 2 - Hot (Blue wire)
- 3 - Cold (White wire)

TRS 1/4"

- Ground to the body of the tip
- Hot (blue wires) straight up the middle
- Cold (white wires) on the little top piece

DB25

DB25's are super fun to make they're just very time consuming.

- Get an 8-channel snake and solder to the points on the previous page.

Here's a comparison on cost for a few cables vs. the cost of their materials:

DB25 to XLRF BREAKOUT (50 FT.)
ONLINE - $499 DIY = $164.06

- Canare MR202-8AT Twisted Pair 8-Channel Audio Cable (2.50/foot x 50= $125)
- Db25 tip w/metal hood $10
- 8 Female Neutrik Tips ($3.70 each x 8= $29.06)

XLR CABLE w/ BRAIDED SHIELDING (25 FT.)
ONLINE - $45 DIY = $21.79

- Canare L-4E6S Star Quad Cable ($0.59/foot= $14.75)
- Neutrik NC3MXX XLR Male Connector - $3.34
- Neutrik NC3FXX XLR Female Connector - $3.70

BRAIDED VS. WOUND SHIELDING

Cables made with braided shielding last longer and have better protections against RFI (Radio Frequency Interference). Over time the wound shielding will unwind and leave gaps. Braided shielding will remain intact if taken care of. **Learn how to properly wind cables** and they will last forever.

I used to think that The Grammy Awards was just major labels having a wank, turns out the awards show is only a small part of the picture. The organization that hosts the Grammys is called The Recording Academy. The Grammys were never either Julia's or my scene/world/scope of influence. Pop music is its own thing for celebrities and that wasn't anything we cared about. When we were recording *In Echo*, the idea of winning a Grammy came up in the conversation and we were like what the hell let's try and we both became Recording Academy members. We found out the organization does a lot for independent musicians, and the reason it has its stigma is because people like us have a skewed perspective.

To become a member, you'll need a recommendation from two current members and pay a membership fee of $150/year. Once you're a member, you can submit your work for consideration, and vote for the Grammy nominees. Those fees also help pay for:

• Year-round advocacy work to help pass legislation that benefits music creators

• MusiCares' health and human services supporting music people in need

• The Grammy Museum's music preservation and education initiatives

• Mentorship and internship programs

The Recording Academy advocates for independent musicians and works with members of Congress to help with everything from protection against AI to tax breaks to increased streaming wages to ticketing reforms. Regardless of whether you want to get involved, you can still take advantage of the services they provide for everyone in the music business.

MUSICARES

www.musicares.org

MusiCares, a part of the Recording Academy, provides critical health and welfare services to musicians, songwriters, engineers, producers, live crew, tour bus drivers, managers, agents, A&R, makeup artists, costume designers, music video creatives & technicians, and anyone whose livelihood depends on music.

MusiCares provides crisis relief, preventive care, recovery resources and need-based financial assistance in three key areas:

• **Mental Health & Addiction Recovery Services**, helping pay for drug rehab and therapy.

• **Health Services** for assistance with medical, dental and vision expenses.

• **Human Services** for need-based financial assistance for basic living expenses like rent, utilities, car payments and insurance premiums, assistance with instrument replacement/

repair if stolen or damaged in a natural disaster, and funeral costs for a music professional or their family member.

THE HITS ACT

In 2025, thanks to The Recording Academy and four bipartisan congress members, the HITS (Help Independent Tracks Succeed) Act was passed. The HITS Act allows independent musicians to write off up to $150,000 of studio costs on their taxes. Ask your accountant or your mom about how you can utilize this tax write-off.

PROTECTION AGAINST AI

The Recording Academy is trying to protect music creators against AI by proposing the following to lawmakers in DC:

- **The NO FAKES Act (Nurture Originals, Foster Art, and Keep Entertainment Safe)** - Preventing unauthorized use of artists' voice, image, and likeness through AI-generated replicas.
- **The TRAIN Act (Transparency and Responsibility for Artificial Intelligence Networks)** - Ensuring creators know when their work is used to train AI systems and can hold companies accountable.
- **The CLEAR Act (Copyright Labeling and Ethical AI Reporting)** - Requiring companies to disclose their use of copyrighted work to train generative AI models.

THE PACE ACT

Currently passed in Maryland, the PACE Act (Protecting Artist's Creative Expression) is part of a nationwide effort to restrict the use of song lyrics as evidence in criminal cases.

DON'T FEED THE TROLLS

One thing people hate to see is other people's success. One thing people love to see is a successful person's demise. When you're in the public eye, you'll most likely have to deal with some sort of trolling. Trolls come in many shapes and sizes. Well, in English it's more specifically twenty six shapes and sizes. The alphabet is rearranged into pernicious prose used to attack an individual or organization online.

Trolls find any reason to humiliate and shame their victims. They rely on the naivete of the general public to believe that what they're claiming is worth engaging in similar conduct towards a target. This can snowball into loss of reputation, job and even suicide. All trolls are bullies, but not all bullies are trolls. Bullies are dicks in person, which means they still have the chance of getting their asses kicked. Troll bullying is also known as *cyberbullying*, meaning it's contained online. They can operate anonymously, sometimes with fake accounts, using VPN (virtual private network) and encrypted email services like ProtonMail, making them impossible to trace. A few thumb taps can destroy a life.

Depending on your perspective, trolls can be terrorists, heroes or anything in between. Whatever reasons people have for becoming a troll, it's usually based on some sort of vigilante-ism, like they think they're doing something good for humanity. There might be some subconscious survival mechanisms at work, trying to thin the herd to keep resources from being depleted or something. It might be a dominance thing, an insecurity, unresolved childhood trauma, legitimate mental illness, one of the four motivation categories that intelligence agencies use to understand human behavior: Money, Ideology, Coercion, Ego (MICE). Or they could just be dicks. Politicians troll each other constantly; these are known as *smear campaigns*. Not a fan of smear campaigns.

The media can be a troll too, printing things that aren't true or thoroughly fact checked. In 2023, Fox News lost a defamation suit and had to pay $787.5 million to Dominion Voting Systems for claiming that their voting machines were used to rig the 2020 election. This was the largest defamation suit in U.S. history. The court papers are an interesting read if you have the time.

If you're releasing music and in the public eye, you're a target for criticism, harassment and trolling. The best advice for dealing with trolls we ever got is:

DON'T FEED THE TROLLS

Do not engage! Any response will be used against you. After a while they will get bored and scurry off to something else. On rare occasions, an unbalanced super fan can become a troll and find a food source (justification for trolling). This is a dangerous situation. Under these special circumstances a regular troll can mutate into a full-blown stalker. These rampaging super trolls don't just target a victim; they target everyone having anything to do with their victim. This means any support bands, venues and sponsors that associate with their target will be harassed and threatened incessantly, sometimes for years on end. We've seen it and it ain't pretty. Nobody is safe when a troll goes berzerk. So if you see a troll scratchin' on your door do NOT open it and do NOT feed it! If things get really bad or you need a media training coach, contact a crisis PR company or a private investigator.

In the US, harassment is protected under the first amendment because it is considered freedom of speech. The police can't help unless it includes threats of violence or bodily harm. Slander isn't illegal but it is actionable, which means you have to hire a lawyer at your own expense. Anonymous trolls are impossible to sue and, in our experience, reporting harassment to social media companies goes completely ignored. The only thing they will respond to is trademark or copyright infringement. If a troll is using your copyrighted material against you, file a trademark claim.

It's very easy to become a troll yourself! Trolls rely on knee-jerk reactions so commenting, reposting, liking, or even believing the claims of a troll helps their cause. Freedom of speech is a right, but that doesn't mean there might not be consequences to bashing a colleague. How you choose to represent yourself online is all on you. Think twice before chiming in, one comment or post can easily destroy a relationship or your reputation. Think of the post button as a trigger on a gun pointed straight at your own foot.

I don't know much about manifestation, but I do know about hard work. Life is like surfing, look where you want to go and you'll head in that direction. Keep your creative brain engaged and concentrate on making your ideas into reality. Over time your body of work will grow and your style will develop. Never stop learning and never stop pushing yourself. Even the most mundane exercises like SEO will cultivate discipline, increase your stamina and sharpen your focus, giving you a better chance of success.

The more you can do yourself, the more money you keep, the better chance you have of making this lifestyle sustainable. The music business is constantly changing but the fundamentals will always stay the same:

Release music, play shows, sell merch.

Success comes in many forms so keep an open mind, work hard and good things will happen. Good luck!

ABOUT THE AUTHORS

We met in 2012 while on tour with our bands (Julia with The Coathangers and Scott with The Growlers) while performing at a festival in Dallas, TX. We are married and live in Long Beach, CA, where we work out of our home studio Centre of Mental Arts (COMA). We have various music projects, including Soft Palms and Julia, Julia. We founded a nonprofit called Studios For Schools, an organization dedicated to providing schools with recording and production equipment. We organize a community music festival called Happy Sundays, which was dubbed the *anti-music festival* by the Los Angeles Times. We co-founded TheMouth.tv, an independent AI-free music video channel and resources for musicians.

hearjuliajulia.com
scottwmontoya.com
softpalmsmusic.com
happysundaysfest.com
studiosforschools.org
themouth.tv

Photo by Jess Giles